T0288204

100
GREATEST
SCIENTISTS

www.royalcollins.com

The 100th Anniversary of
China's Water Conservancy Collection

(VOLUME I)

100 GREATEST SCIENTISTS

Edited by Wu Zhongru, Tang Hongwu, Xu Hui, and Guo Jichao

Translated by Xuemeng Angela Li

RC

Books Beyond Boundaries

ROYAL COLLINS

The 100th Anniversary of China's Water Conservancy Collection (Volume I):
100 Greatest Scientists

Edited by Wu Zhongru, Tang Hongwu, Xu Hui, and Guo Jichao
Translated by Xuemeng Angela Li

First published in 2023 by Royal Collins Publishing Group Inc.
Groupe Publication Royal Collins Inc.
BKM Royalcollins Publishers Private Limited

Headquarters: 550-555 boul. René-Lévesque O Montréal (Québec) H2Z1B1 Canada
India office: 805 Hemkunt House, 8th Floor, Rajendra Place, New Delhi 110008

Original Edition © Hohai University Press

ISBN: 978-1-4878-1098-6

To find out more about our publications, please visit www.royalcollins.com.

EDITORIAL BOARD

CONTENTS

FOREWORD

One hundred years is just a short moment in the course of time, but it is also a long journey in the history of human society. More than 4,000 years ago, Emperor Yu started the civilizational history of the Chinese people prosper the country with water regulation. Since then, successive generations of Yu's descendants have been working to develop water conservancy and eliminate floods to inherit and promote the undertakings, which left enormous stories of water regulation and set up countless monuments for water regulation. Names including Emperor Yu, Sunshu Ao, Ximen Bao, and Li Bing were as brilliant as stars, shining brightly in the sky of China. Famous water conservancy projects such as Anfengtang Reservoir, Zhengguo Canal, Yinzhang Shi'er Canals, Dujiangyan, and the Grand Canal are not only recorded in the glorious history of Chinese civilization but are also still benefiting the world after thousands of years.

As the wheel of history entered the modern era, a group of hydraulic professionals such as Li Yizhi, Zheng Zhaojing, Wang Huzhen, and Zhang Hanying inherited the ancient Chinese water regulation experience, on the basis of which they actively absorbed the technological achievements of modern civilization and opened a new chapter of modern Chinese water conservancy. After the founding of the People's Republic of China, as the foundation of the national economy, water conservancy witnessed rapid development and brilliant achievements under the leadership of the Party and the State. In addition to the radical cure of floods in major rivers, a large number of mega projects emerged from the Gezhouba Dam, Three Gorges Project, to the Yellow River Xiaolangdi Dam, etc. These projects transformed natural disasters into water resources and created comprehensive practical benefits through flood control, irrigation, power generation, navigation, and tourism.

The calmness of rivers that can be witnessed by the world and recorded in history has long been a long-cherished dream of the Chinese people, and it can only be realized under the leadership of the Communist Party of China. 2021 marked the 100th anniversary of the founding of the Communist Party of China. The development of modern Chinese water conservancy has been going on for more than 100 years. In order to reflect on the past, follow up on past masters' wisdom, inherit the Chinese civilization of water regulation, and promote the spirit of water conservancy and the spirit of China, Hohai University organized and planned *The 100th Anniversary of China's Water Conservancy Collection*.

The collection includes two volumes: *100 Greatest Projects* and *100 Greatest Scientists*.

100 Greatest Projects selected 100 typical hydraulic projects of China and provided readers with a comprehensive understanding of the century-long arduous development course of China's hydraulic projects and their glorious achievements through the introduction of the development, construction management, and economic and social benefits of the projects. The volume also took into account the uniqueness of different hydraulic projects and selected different types of projects, including hydropower projects, water diversion projects, flood diversion projects, large-scale irrigation districts, dive projects, and port projects. It also introduced a large number of typical projects with their own characteristics, such as the Jinping-I Dam, Three Gorges, Longtan Hydropower Station, and other world's largest hydroelectric dams, including the Xin'anjiang Hydropower Station, the first large hydropower station in China that was surveyed, designed and constructed domestically.

100 Greatest Scientists was mainly composed of the glorious achievements of some academicians and experts (born before 1949) in the fields of water conservancy, hydropower, and water transportation. The book introduced the readers to the hydraulic scientists of modern China over the past hundred years, who studied both in the East and the West world and obtained achievements connecting the past and the present. Following the spirit of Emperor Yu and having the magnificent wish to regulate and develop rivers, they built dams, power stations, ports, and docks with efforts and wisdom. They built irrigation areas, dredged rivers and canals, and obtained extraordinary achievements in various aspects, including water conservancy, hydropower, water transportation, etc. They held the belief that "I do not have to be credited to success but must contribute my parts to it." They have acted with dedication and selflessness. They had always been chasing after the brightness in their heart regardless of the difficulties with the fire of their ideal of fighting for the water conservancy undertakings constantly burning.

Reflect on the past, and look forward to the future. Regulating water to benefit people has been a significant undertaking for thousands of years. The majestic dams are the witness to the prosperity of the world. Water is always closely related to people's livelihood. It is hydraulic professionals' and departments' responsibility and mission to consolidate the foundation of water security, enhance people's well-being, and constantly improve people's sense of achievement, happiness, and security.

Currently, the situation of China's water security is still serious. Hydraulic professionals must implement General Secretary Xi Jinping's new ideas, thinking, and requirements on water regulation and prosperity, which is to "prioritize water conservation, balance the space, regulate systematically, and utilize both the state and the market's functions." They must coordinate the work between water disaster prevention and control, water conservation, water ecological protection and restoration, water environment control, etc., to constantly accelerate the upgrading of watershed protection and governance system, improve the flood prevention and mitigation system, comprehensive utilization of water resources system, water ecological and environmental protection system, comprehensive management system of watershed, and spare no efforts to protect national water security.

Over the past hundred years, the development of China's water conservancy undertakings has witnessed the course of the Communist Party of China leading the Chinese people to prosperity and prosperity. It recorded how the great national projects protected the peace of rivers, advanced economic development, and created a better life. During this century, hydraulic professionals endured difficulties, only to focus on national rejuvenation. During this century, hydraulic professionals never forgot their original intention and were only devoted to the well-being of the people. All their names will shine forever in the history of China's water conservancy construction and development, representing the spirit of water conservancy and national pillar. All these majestic water conservancy projects, standing magnificently in the rivers, are symbols of national power and people's wisdom, highlighting the spirit and confidence of China.

The spirit of Emperor Yu includes a sense of charity, the spirit of fighting, the pursuit of innovation, a scientific attitude, and open-mindedness. The lives and deeds of generations of outstanding hydraulic professionals are the most vivid portrayal of the "Spirit of Emperor Yu." All the major hydraulic projects are eternal monuments of China's practice of water regulation following Emperor Yu, and will always be a source of strength and models for future generations.

The 100th Anniversary of China's Water Conservancy Collection is a beneficial attempt to tell the story of Chinese hydraulic professionals, to promote the spirit of water conservancy, the spirit of China, and to show the power and confidence of China. It is not only suitable for the theme of the era but also of realistic significance. We hope that this series will be seeds that continue to sprout, blossom, and bear fruit until eventually become a great spectacle.

EDITORIAL GROUP
February 2021

WU TONGJU

A Helpful and Benevolent Figure

In 1906, Haizhou was flooded. Wu Tongju "witnessed the disastrous situation, wondered the cause for a flood of such seriousness." He urgently collected various maps and was ready to create a complete map of the state waterway for study purposes. "The seriousness of the flood" had strengthened his faith in a career in water conservancy to benefit his hometown.

WU TONGJU (1871–1944), who styled himself "Xiafeng," "Liangxuan," and "Yichen" too, was from Nancheng Town, Guanyun County in Haizhou (now Lianyungang, Jiangsu). He was a famous expert in hydraulics from the late Qing Dynasty to the Republic of China era and the earliest Chinese expert who studied water conservancy issues of the Yi, Shu, and Si basins.

Wu Tongju's ancestors lived in Taoyuan County of Hunan Province and later moved to the Nancheng Town in Haizhou to serve as generals guarding the town. He grew up in a poor family during his teen years. To make a living, he put great efforts into studying and achieved success and fame eagerly.

Wu Tongju

Wu Tongju was appointed as a state magistrate directly affiliated with Haizhou. He was in charge of grain transportation, irrigation, and water conservancy affairs. In 1904, he became the director and the chief chairman of academic affairs of Haizhou Inducing Institute concurrently, during which he carried out the angle measurement of the Haizhou map and turned the measurement results into lithographic printing. In 1914, he participated in the investigation of Haizhou port and wrote *A Guide to Surveying Haizhou Port*, which provided valuable data for selecting the Longhai railway's routes and locating the port.

Wu Tongju was once a member of China's first geographical academic group, the Chinese Geographical Society. He also served as the editor-in-chief of the *Journal of Jiangsu Water Conservancy Association*. He wrote extensive works and published many articles, such as "Explanation of The Huai River Diagram," "An Attempting Discussion of Guiding Huai River into the Sea," "A Systematic Review of Transforming the Grand Canal into Water Channel," and so on.

In 1923, Wu Tongju served as the Director of Jiangsu Provincial Water Resources Agency, mainly responsible for water conservancy affairs across the province. He also served as an instructor at Nanjing Hohai Engineering Specialized School (now Hohai University), teaching Chinese then water conservancy history. During this period, Wu Tongju wrote *The Huai River System Timeline Full Edition*, which systematically reflected both the ancient and modern features of the Huai River basin and elaborated on the water conservancy and flood of the river. The book played an important role as a reference in the Huai River water control project after the founding of New China.

In 1928, Wu Tongju went to Nanjing to serve as the Second Division Chief of Jiangsu Provincial Department of Construction, and the member and secretary of the Grand Canal Project Rehabilitation Committee, where he later became an inspector. During his appointment, he participated in the compilation of *A Complete Book of Jiangsu Province's Water Conservancy*. Later, the compilation of the Editorial Committee was suspended due to the lack of funding. Wu Tongju believed the book was of great significance and decided to continue writing it himself. After a total of 10 years of hardworking writing, with seven editions and 43 volumes, *A Complete Book of Jiangsu Province's Water Conser-*

Photo of *A Complete Book of Jiangsu Province's Water Conservancy*

vancy was finally completed. It has also become a monograph of water conservancy history with unprecedented scale in Jiangsu Province's history. The book has great value in reference and research, particularly for developing water conservancy in East China. In addition, the materials compiled in *A Complete Book of Jiangsu Province's Water Conservancy* were not limited to Jiangsu and the time of writing. It involves the origin, evolution, advantage, and disadvantage of a variety of water conservancy projects in East China, including Huai River, Grand Canal, Jiangnan Canal, Tai Lake Basin, Jiangnan Haitang Li Lower River, and salt reclamation area, Yi, Shu, Si Basin at the north of Huai River, etc. It was known as the "vault of East China's water conservancy data."

Many of the data in Wu Tongju's hydraulics works were from his self-made measuring tools, self-carried measuring instrument, records measured on foot, and hand-drawn maps of Jiangsu's water channels. It provided the most authentic and valuable water conservancy documents for the later generations to build the port. Wu Tongju conducted in-depth research on guiding the Huai River, dividing the Yishu River, regulating canals, and harnessing the Yellow River, Yangtze River, and other rivers. He formed his own thoughts on water conservancy, which was full of sparkling ideas and had left precious historical data for studying water conservancy history in China. It also played an important role in the construction of water conservancy projects in New China, with significance in reference and guidance to this day.

LI YIZHI

One Generation's Sage of Water and Water Conservancy Pioneer

During Li Yizhi's adolescence, Chinese people were suffering from troubles both domestically and internationally. He cared for the country and its citizens with great enthusiasm for saving China with science since his early childhood. He studied twice in Germany and always achieved top rankings in class. But he didn't graduate with a degree. He said, "I came all the way to Germany for knowledge, not a degree. Moreover, I am a government-sponsored student whose expenses are covered by the citizens. Even one cent has to be saved, and wasting is unacceptable no matter what." He taught his students, "To complete great works, not to become great officials. To be pragmatic in everything, not to chase after fame." and "Young people who study engineering should start developing the willingness to benefit the people and world as a student, so that when they reflect on what they have learned daily, they can constantly think of how to benefit the general public."

Li Yizhi

LI YIZHI (1882–1938), whose given name was "Xie" and styled himself "Yicheng." He was born in Pucheng, Shanxi Province. He was a water conservancy expert, educator, pioneer, and founder of modern water conservancy in China.

Li Yizhi was smart from a young age and was particularly good at mathematics. In 1909, he graduated from the Imperial University of Peking and was admitted to the Department of Civil Engineering of Berlin Institute of Technology in Germany. He came back to China in 1911, returned to Germany two years later, and traveled to many countries in Europe. After investigating the modern water conservancy projects in Europe, he deeply felt that China's water conservancy fell behind. He transferred to Danzig University in Berlin and majored in hydraulics instead.

After returning to China in 1915, Yichang Li served as the Dean and Professor of Nanjing Hohai Engineering Specialized School (now Hohai University), the first institution of hydraulic higher education in China founded by Zhang Jian. Educating students at the school, which was located right next to Qingliang Mountain, he successfully trained a large number of modern China's earliest hydraulic engineering professionals, including Song Xishang, Sha Yuqing, Wang Huzhen, etc. He had made tremendous groundbreaking contributions to the educational cause of hydraulic engineering in modern China. He complied and wrote textbooks himself, such as *Hydraulic Engineering, Hydraulic Engineering Experiments, Practical Hydraulics*, etc. Following his advocation, the school led the compilation of some classic textbooks that were widely spread in public, filling in the blank in hydraulic education at the time. He translated a variety of foreign hydraulic monographs, actively introduced advanced western hydraulic technology, and initiated many hydraulic professional terms that are still in use now. He also attached great importance to summarizing the water control experience of the ancient working class of our country. He connected the knowledge from China and the western world while researching and teaching his students hydraulic engineering. He also extensively collected both Chinese and western books on river regulation and made various river engineering models while he paid great attention to creating opportunities for students to practice. He often took students to different rivers and reached for field visits.

Canal Head of Jinhui Canal

Li Yizhi was a doer in water conservancy who benefited the entire society. In 1922, he left Hohai Engineering Specialized School and returned to his hometown in Shaanxi Province, where he served as Director of Shaanxi Water Conservancy Bureau and Chief Engineer of Weibei Hydraulic Engineering Bureau. The famous water diversion and irrigation project "Eight Irrigation Districts in Guanzhong" was led and planned by him during this period. The Jinghui[1] canal project led by him is the first large-scale irrigation project constructed utilizing modern science and technology.

Li Yizhi was the pioneer of transforming Chinese water conservancy from traditional to modern era. He was the founder of modern hydraulic science and technology in China. He established the first water resources laboratory and the first hydraulic laboratory in China. When he served as the chairman and chief engineer of the Yellow River Conservancy Committee, he advocated the concurrent development of the upper, middle, and lower reaches. He proposed the general plan and specific measures for regulating the Yellow River. He was the first water conservancy expert who brought up the idea of "comprehensive water control."

Li Yizhi devoted his whole life to the undertakings of China's water conservancy. As he lay dying, he still repeatedly stated, "We should look forward to the new generation and continue working on the river regulation following my simple will with scientific approaches and discussions by steps. For water conservancy projects that were still in progress or hadn't started, manpower and financial resources shall be exhausted to complete them over a short period of time."

---

1. Translator's Note (TN): "hui" means the benefits of Jing River in Chinese.

HU BUCHUAN

Who Established Himself to Live up to Yu and His Descendants

"To contribute to China's water conservancy and benefit the people; if the people are rich, so does the country; if the people are strong, so does the country." This idea was deeply integrated into Hu Buchuan's thoughts and actions, which made him devote his whole life to the undertakings of water conservancy and realized his ideal of benefiting the people. Inspired by his teacher Mr. Li Yizhi's spirit to care about the country and benefit the people, he followed him to develop water conservancy projects in Shaanxi Province. After Li Yizhi passed away, Hu Buchuan still "remained at his position" and firmly carried "the responsibility of canal protection." Some of the projects he led have been in use until now, which "continuously benefit the people." Hu Buchuan always kept the initial intention of "establish oneself to live up to Yu and his descendants, encourage oneself to overcome hardships" in mind. The water conservancy projects he followed Mr. Li Yizhi to develop and the ones he built in his hometown Linhai during his adolescence and declining years were all witnesses of his extraordinary water conservancy career and what his noble feelings linked to.

Hu Buchuan (1893–1981), whose given name was Zhengguo and styled himself Zhuming and Buchuan. He was a water conservancy expert born in Linhai, Zhejiang Province. He served in a variety of positions, including the engineer and survey team leader of Shaanxi Weibei Water Conservancy Project Bureau, chief engineer of Hanzhong Water Conservancy Project Office, engineer of North China Water Resources Committee, chief engineer of Xijiang Sluice Construction, and chief engineer of Jinqing Sluice Engineering Office, etc. In 1957, Hu Buchuan became the first director of the Institute of Water Conservancy History of the China Institute of Hydropower and Water Resources Research of the Ministry of Hydropower.

Hu Buchuan

When Hu Buchuan was young, his hometown suffered from flood that frequently inundated the crops. The idea of studying water conservancy thus sprouted in him. In 1917, Hu Buchuan was admitted to Nanjing Hohai Engineering Specialized School. During his time there, he was appreciated by Mr. Li Yizhi because of his studious and down-to-earth qualities and thus became one of the students that Mr. Li Yizhi was most proud of. After graduation, he stayed in the school as a teaching assistant and served as the editor of the school journal concurrently. A year later, Hu Buchuan was invited by Mr. Li Yizhi to participate in water conservancy development in Shaanxi Province.

Hu Buchuan has dedicated his life to undertakings in water conservancy. He followed Mr. Li Yizhi and served as the leader of the hydrologic survey team of Weibei Water Conservancy Project Bureau in Shaanxi Province. He investigated the hydrologic and geographical landscape of Jing River and planned the construction of the Jinghui Canal. Later, he was ordered to survey in Hanzhong, design, and implement the Hanhui Canal Project, during which he drowned three times while surveying the Yellow River. But he did not back down at all and continued to draw the hydrograph. Later, due to the turbulent political situation at the time, Hu Buchuan was stuck in Nanjing when he tried to return to his hometown. Because of Mr. Li Yizhi's calling and caring for northwestern China's water conservancy projects, Hu Buchuan returned to Shaanxi again and devoted himself to the construction of Wei Canal and Luo Canal. Projects funds were in

Photo of Old Jinqing Sluice

extreme shortage due to the special stage of the country, with Mr. Li Yizhi passing away soon after. Faced with difficulties and grief, Mr. Hu Buchuan remembered the instructions of his teacher and completed the canal construction project. After years of arduous construction, eight canals, including Meihui Canal, Hanhui Canal, Weihui Canal, and others were completed. Since then, the 800 miles long Qinchuan was no longer disturbed by drought and harvested wheat and cotton instead.

No matter how great the achievements were, Hu Buchuan had always been concerned about his hometown and never forgot about the construction there. After learning that his hometown aimed to develop water conservancy, he resolutely gave up the high-paying job to be an engineer at North China Water Conservancy Committee and returned to his hometown. He took the position as chief engineer of Jinqing Sluice Engineering Division to design and build Jinqing Sluice with a low salary. Jinqing sluice is one of China's first medium-to-large sized self-designed and self-constructed sluices.

During the construction of Jinqing Sluice, he was also responsible for the construction of Huangyan's Xi River sluice as an engineer. The construction of Jinqing Sluice and Xi River Sluice is a milestone in the development of modern Chinese water conservancy as it's the start of the Chinese water conservancy history of domestically designed and built large-scale sluice. After Hu Buchuan retired and went back to his hometown, he paid attention to water conservancy and education there, made several donations to build schools, and helped construct dams and berms to benefit the villagers.

ZHENG ZHAOJING

The Pioneer of Modern Water Conservancy

Zheng Zhaojing devoted himself to the construction of water conservancy with full enthusiasm, contributed his knowledge to the water conservancy undertakings without reservation, and strived for China's hydraulic science for nearly 70 years. In his declining years, Zheng continued to fight at the frontier of water conservancy, working long hours daily. Whenever his family asked him to take more rest, he always said seriously, "I don't have much time left. I need to seize this limited time and complete more works for the Four Modernizations." Zheng Zhaojing swore to dedicate his life to the motherland. His patriotic spirit of selfless devotion to the country is a precious spiritual wealth for future generations.

ZHENG ZHAOJING (1894–1989) styled himself Shubo and Henglu. He was a water conservancy expert from Taixing in Jiangsu Province. He founded the National Bureau of Hydraulic Research, the first research institute of modern hydraulic scientific experiments in China, and the Department of Hydraulic Engineering of National Central University. He served as the chief professor of Hydraulics at the Hohai University of Engineering and the interim dean of the Engineering School of Tongji University.

Zheng Zhaojing

Zheng Zhaojing received good formative education from a young age. As a teenager, he witnessed with his own eyes how people lived miserably after the Yellow River burst and overflew. This has inspired his magnificent ambition of "revitalizing water conservancy and saving the country scientifically" and strengthened his ideal and belief of striving to explore and dedicate to the country. In 1912, Zheng Zhaojing was admitted to the preparatory school of Nanjing University of Law and Political Science and later transferred to the Engineering School of Tongji University. He was also recommended to study in Germany with the best grade among his peers. He was one of the first students to study modern hydraulic technology in Germany. While studying overseas, he devoted himself to studying modern western science, discussing the principle of river regulation, and mastering the technology of hydraulic model tests. He also brought back the research results of his tutor to China. He translated them into the Chinese version named *Discussion on Regulating the Yellow River*, which drew different parties' attention.

After Zheng Zhaojing graduated, he gave up the wealthy lifestyle overseas and returned to China. He engaged in hydraulic construction for a long term and made important contributions to China's hydraulic science. Zheng Zhaojing introduced the modern hydraulic model test technology from Germany and established the Central Hydraulic Experiment Institute (now Nanjing Hydraulic Research Institute), the first research institute of modern hydraulic science experimental in China. He also founded Panxi,

Shimen, Wugong Hydraulic Laboratory, and Geotechnical Laboratory, etc., which completed tremendous ground-breaking work for the development of the hydraulic model tests, geotechnical test, and hydrologic survey in China.

In the 1930s, China fell behind in hydraulic construction, and floods frequently occurred in river basins. After learning that severe flood disasters took place in the Yangtze-Huai River Basin, Zheng Zhao personally went to Jiangdu, Gaoyou, and other places with on-site guidance for disaster relief. In 1938, the dike at Huayuankou of the Yellow River burst. In the sight of danger, Zheng Zhao was appointed to measure the data of the burst breach, carry out the flood drainage test, and rehabilitate of the Yellow River flood to block the breach, drain the gap, and consolidate the dike. He also presided over the municipal construction and long-term planning of Shanghai, port planning of Qingdao, and participated in the construction of many hydraulic infrastructures in China.

Nanjing Hydraulic Research Institute

Zheng Zhaojing not only devoted himself to the research and advancement of hydraulics, but also started the history of Chinese self-manufactured instruments. In the 1930s, China's engineering measuring instruments were all imported. Because of the turbulent political situation at the time, it was difficult to repair and reuse the instruments once malfunction happened. Procuring new instruments was even more difficult. Under the leadership of Zheng Zhaojing, the first hydraulic instrument manufacturing factory was established in China. Through the disassembly and careful research of foreign instruments, the technical personnel of the factory could not only repair hydraulic instruments, but also manufacture optical measuring instruments, becoming the largest domestic supplier of measuring instruments.

Zheng Zhaoxing, who deeply cared about water conservancy, had never stopped writing throughout his entire life. He is the author of *River Engineering, Canal Engineering, Harbour Engineering, Water Conservancy History of China, Water Conservancy of China, Urban Planning, Hydrology*, etc. In his book *Science and Civilization in China*, Dr. Joseph Needham said, "Without referring to Zheng Zhaojing's *River Engineering* and *History of Water Conservancy in China*, it would be impossible for me to write the part about water conservancy projects."

WANG HUZHEN

The Father of China's Multi-arch Dam

"In the past, only corn was stored in a warehouse; now, so does rainwater. With stored water to relieve draught and generate electricity, the grain will produce an abundant harvest, and numerous trades will become wealthy." When Wang Huzhen studied at Hohai Engineering Specialized School in 1915, his mentor, Mr. Li Yizhen, asked the students to give a Chinese name to "reservoir." Wang Huzhen thought of the word "Shuiku"[1] and wrote the above poem. The creation of this term fully demonstrated the wisdom of young Wang Huzhen, and the beautiful vision expressed in this poem was realized through the dedication and efforts of him and generations of hydraulic professionals in New China.

WANG HUZHEN (1897–1989), a hydraulic expert from Jiaxing, Zhejiang Province, was one of the pioneers of modern hydraulic engineering technology in China. He was an academician of the Chinese Academy of Sciences, former consultant, and first-class engineer of the Ministry of Water Resources. He was praised as the "Father of China's multi-arch dam" by the hydraulic field.

Wang Huzhen graduated from Nanjing Hohai Engineering Specialized School (now Hohai University) in 1917 and obtained a master's degree from Cornell University in 1923. In 1950, Wang Huzhen served as the director

Wang Huzhen

of the Huai River Regulation Committee's engineering department, presided over Huai River regulation's technical work, and was responsible for the design and construction. He built Foziling Reservoir Dam, the first large-scale reinforced concrete multi-arch dam project in China and Asia. The project opened a new era of multi-arch dam in the history of hydraulic construction in China. In 1954, under the leadership of Wang Huzhen, the Huai River Regulation Committee built the Meishan Reservoir Multi-arch buttress dam, for which the dam construction technology in China reached an advanced level globally. In 1956, Wang Huzhen was the chief engineer of the Sanmenxia hydro-electric complex project, the first large-scale water conservancy project built on the trunk stream of the Yellow River. He was responsible for constructing and developing the Sanmenxia Reservoir too.

Wang Huzhen also made great achievements in academic research. During the construction of hydraulics, hydropower, railway, coal systems, and other types of projects, mechanical analysis of underground cavern is the most tedious work. It was not only time-consuming but also error-prone. Therefore, Wang Huzhen wrote *Structural Design of Underground Cavern* and *Design Theory and*

---

1. TN: It means the warehouse of water in Chinese.

Foziling Reservoir Multi-arch Dam

Calculation of Hydraulic Tunnel. He also edited the *Modern Engineering Mathematics Manual* of five more million words. The manual was one of the few large-scale reference books in China.

Wang Huzhen trained a large number of construction talents for China's water conservancy undertakings. He taught at his alma mater, Hohai Engineering Specialized School and Zhejiang University during different stages. When the Foziling Reservoir was built, there was a shortage of talents. He led a group of intellectuals to learn by doing there. He sent the books he brought back from abroad to the library, where everyone rushed to borrow them. He also personally taught courses such as "General Design Principles of Dam Construction" and "Preliminary Design of Foziling Multi-arch Dam." Thus, everyone called the construction site "Foziling University" and affectionately called him the president. At that time, this "university" trained a new generation of talents, including Zhu Bofang, Cao Chusheng, Cao Hongxun, Zhu Qifeng, and so on. In 1960, Wang Huzhen was appointed as the president of Beijing Water Conservancy Hydropower College. He worked hard, dedicated himself to the cause of water conservancy education, and made great contributions.

ZHANG HANYING

"The Yellow River's Calling is Where My Heart Lies"

In June 1949, Zhang Hanying went to Kaifeng to serve as the consultant of the Yellow River Conservancy Committee of the Liberated Area. The fall of the year was hot, and the flood season was to arrive. He was deeply impressed by the fresh atmosphere, busy scene, efficient work, capable style, and high sense of responsibility of the staff at this commission that the people led. He was particularly impressed when knowing that during the flood control meeting, the Yellow River Conservancy Committee of the Liberated Area decided that for the flood control work of the year, it would guarantee that "When the Yellow River flow in Shan County rises to 16,000 cubic meters per second, the levee in the lower reaches will not burst." No one had ever dared to guarantee that the Yellow River levee would not burst! The rocket-high courage of the Communist Party of China left Zhang Hanying shocked and impressed. He deeply felt that the world had changed greatly. But at the same time, he was very excited. Because in such an unprecedented new era, he would definitely find his own position and realize his long-standing dream of the Yellow River by working for the people-led Yellow River regulation team.

ZHANG HANYING (1900–2002), who styled himself Huafu, was born in Heze, Shandong Province. He was a member of the Communist Party of China and a hydraulic expert. He was also one of the pioneers of China's modern water conservancy undertakings who made significant contributions, particularly to the regulation and development of the Yellow River.

In 1921, he was admitted to the waitlist of an overseas study program sponsored by Shandong Province. He went to study at the Civil Engineering Department of the University of Illinois in the United States that summer. He then graduated with an honorable completion certificate and a bachelor's degree in civil engineering. Later, he went for graduate studies at Cornell University for a year, graduated with a master's degree in civil engineering, then returned home in 1925.

Zhang Hanying

After the founding of the People's Republic of China, he finally realized his long-cherished wish for many years, which was to regulate the Yellow River. In 1953, the Northwest Soil and Water Conservation Delegation led by Zhang Hanying carried out an investigation and research in key areas of the Loess Plateau through an 85-day trip of more than 2000 kilometers and completed the *Report of Northwest Soil and Water Conservation Delegation*. In 1954, the "Yellow River Radical Cure Investigation Group" was established. As a core group member, Zhang Hanying participated in an investigation that lasted 90 days and traveled 12,000 kilometers. The two investigations obtained important first-hand information for the planning of the Yellow River regulation. In the same year, the "Yellow River Planning Commission" was established. As a committee member, Zhang Hanying directly participated in the formulation and approval of the planning.

Canal Head of People's Victory Canal

During his years of hydraulic practice, Zhang Hanying accumulated rich experience and academic achievements. He is the author of *Discussion on the River Regulation Strategy of Past Dynasties*, *Introduction to River Regulation in Ming and Qing Dynasties*, and other works.

Zhang Hanying used to serve as the Deputy Minister of the Ministry of Water Resources and the Ministry of Water Resources and Power. He was concurrently the Director of the Technical Committee. He directly participated in the major decisions of water conservancy work of New China, especially regarding the regulation of the Yellow River, in which he suggested comprehensively arranging the upper, middle and lower reaches. He proposed the development of the Yellow River irrigation area and built the People's Victory Canal, which was the first canal to irrigate by diverting the Yellow River in its lower reaches and benefited the farmland in northern Henan through the irrigation of the Yellow River. In 1956, Zhang Hanying was responsible for establishing the China Hydraulic Engineering Association. China's water conservancy development, especially the development of the Yellow River regulation, has made world-renowned achievements that comprise Zhang Hanying's blood, sweat, and tears. He has made groundbreaking contributions to New China's water conservancy undertakings.

In 1981, Zhang Hanying joined the Communist Party of China. The 81-year-old "yellow river elder" wrote, "A anthem of sunset with remaining energy, a loyal heart to keep forward." He still insisted on going to the office every day to study, work, write, greet visitors, and care for the country, water conservancy and the cause of Yellow River regulation from the bottom of his heart.

XU KAI

Whose Personality Was as Clear as Water and Loved His Motherland

Xu Kai, Wang Huzhen, and Zhang Wentian had a good relationship during their time at Hohai Engineering Specialized School. They encouraged and learned from each other in their studies, and all set the development of water conservancy and revitalization of China as a life goal. When he was studying at the University of California, he happened to live with Zhang Wentian and was deeply influenced by Zhang Wentian's advanced thinking, which strengthened his faith in fighting for the revitalization of China and the relief of people's hardship. He cared for his motherland and was determined to clarify and wipe out China's disgrace and revitalize the country. He named his two sons Qinghua, Chenghua.[1]

Xu Kai (1900–1970), who styled himself Jundi, was a native of Wuxi, Jiangsu Province. He was a pioneer in modern water conservancy cause in China, an expert in hydraulic engineering, and an educator of water conservancy.

Xu Kai lived by Lake Tai since he was young. As a teenager, he often saw the villagers have to step on the water wheel arduously to irrigate the farmland by the lake. This made him realize that "water is the foundation of agriculture" from a young age, and he was determined to study water conservancy. In 1915, he was admitted to Nanjing Hohai Engineering Specialized School (now Hohai University).

After graduation, Xu Kai successively worked in Jiangbei Canal Project Bureau and Shunzhi Water Conservancy Committee and later went to work in the United States. He was admitted to the University

Xu Kai

of California in 1922. In 1924, he graduated from the University of California with a master's degree and then returned to China for a life fighting for the undertakings of Chinese water conservancy. Xu Kai completed many on-site surveys, from assisting Mr. Li Yichang to carry out the planning and design of the Jinghui New Irrigation Canal Project in Shaanxi Province to working at the Qiantang River Engineering Bureau. He became one of the first pioneers in modern water conservancy in China.

In 1928, the North China Water Conservancy Commission was established. Xu Kai was appointed as the technical director. In 1927, he went to the site with the most disastrous conditions during the Yongding River flood to investigate and research. He presided over the compilation of *A Plan for Yongding River's Radical Cure*, which was the earliest blueprint of the planning of Huai River Basin and the beginning of river regulation per basin planning. In 1929, Xu Kai joined the Huai River Diversion Committee and participated in the planning and compilation of the *Huai River Diversion Project Plan*. The plan was

---

1. TN: The two names combined together mean "clarify for China" in Chinese literally.

an important technological achievement of China's comprehensive regulation of basin water conservancy in the early 1930s. When Xu Kai was leading the planning and design of the regulation of the North Jiangsu Canal, he proposed to transform the canal with modern technology. He also concurrently served as the director-general of the Project Bureau of the 17th District of Huai River Diversion Commission and the Lixia River Project Bureau, where he presided over the construction of the Huaiyin Water Control Project, the Huaiyin Navigation Lock, the

Old Photo of the construction of Shaobo Navigation lock in 1935

Shaobo Navigation Lock, and the Liulaojian Navigation Lock, which made great contributions to the navigation, irrigation and drainage of the North Jiangsu Province.

At the home front of the Anti-Japanese War, Xu Kai presided over the Qi River Canalization Project's construction, which was particularly exciting during wartime. In addition, under his auspices and planning, the Huai River Diversion Commission also carried out regulation projects of the Chishui River and Wu River waterway on the Yangtze River, which supported and promoted the navigation and transportation at the home front of the Anti-Japanese War. He also attached great importance to the establishment of the national hydrological network and the survey and measurement of the rivers, which served as the technical preparation for the water conservancy construction after the victory of the Anti-Japanese War.

While engaged in project construction and promoting the development of agricultural irrigation, Xu Kai was also committed to cultivating talents. He insisted on giving lectures to students in person when he served as the director of the Department of Hydraulic Engineering of the School of Engineering of the National Central University and trained a group of elites in hydraulics for China's water conservancy undertaking.

After the founding of the People's Republic of China, Xu Kai served as the director of the first technical committee of the Ministry of Water Resources. He and Li Baohua, Deputy Minister of Water Resources at the time, visited different places along the Huai River Basin and put forward the proposal of a "plan for both water storage and drainage," which was adopted as the national policy of the regulation of Huai River.

In 1959, Xu Kai was appointed as the Chief Engineer of the Planning Bureau of the Ministry of Water Resources and Electric Power. He was responsible for the basin planning of major rivers, the construction planning of water conservancy of all provinces and autonomous regions as well as the planning and review of major national water conservancy and hydropower projects. He advocated unified planning by river basin with comprehensive regulation in order to achieve rationalized and scientific strategic layout and decision-making of water conservancy projects. In terms of irrigation and drainage, he made great efforts to advance the irrigation undertakings in New China and studied the issues spotted during the development of agricultural irrigation. His thoughts and achievements in basin planning, irrigation, and drainage technology are valuable experiences and wealth for later generations.

SHI JIAYANG

Who Inherited the Legacy of Tsinghua University

Shi Jiayang chose engineering as his major because he witnessed the beatings of coolies in Shanghai when he was young and thus was determined to take the life path of "save the nation with science and education." To save the nation with science and learn advanced technologies from the West, he was admitted to Tsinghua University's preparatory school for studying in America during the rising "going abroad fever" in China at that time.

SHI JIAYANG (1902–2001) was born in Fuzhou, Fujian Province. He was the founder of Tsinghua University's engineering department, a hydropower scientist, and an educator in engineering.

In 1915, Shi Jiayang was admitted to Tsinghua University's preparatory school for studying in America. From 1923 to 1928, he obtained a bachelor's degree in mechanical engineering, another bachelor's and master's degree in electrical engineering from Massachusetts Institute of Technology, as well as a master's degree in civil engineering from Cornell University. In five years, he studied three majors and graduated with four degrees, demonstrating his strong learning ability and laying a solid foundation for later work in engineering education.

After returning to China in 1928, he taught in the Department of Civil Engineering of Tsinghua University. He later went to the Royal

Shi Jiayang

Research Institute of Hydraulic Engineering and Shipbuilding in Berlin and Karlsruhe Institute of Technology in Germany for further study and visits from 1934 to 1935. During 1955 and 1957, he studied at the Moscow Power Engineering Institute and Leningrad Hydroelectric Design Institute in the Soviet Union. Then between 1957 and 1985, he served as both a professor in the Department of Hydraulic Engineering and the director of the academic research group of water resources planning at Tsinghua University. Since 1986, Shi Jiayang has been appointed as a professor in the Department of Water Resources and Hydraulic Engineering of Tsinghua University.

Shi Jiayang graduated from Tsinghua, then returned and entrenched himself in Tsinghua. He diligently taught and cultivated numerous students and successfully trained generations of excellent Chinese talents in science and technology. He pursued science with a great focus on the experiment. He designed and presided over the construction of the hydraulic laboratory at that time. It supported the model test with a hydraulic turbine test bench set up. It also had an 80-meter-long test tank built outdoors for ship model test and velocity meter correction.

Shi Jiayang paid special attention to the practice of engineering. Even during the Anti-Japanese War, he did not stop his exploration of the great rivers of the motherland and contributed wisdom and strength to the production and safeguard of the home front. When National Southwestern Association University was operating, its School of Engineering and Yunnan Economic Committee jointly organized Yunnan Hydropower Survey Team, which was led and guided by Shi Jiayang. In two years, the team surveyed the water resources of 26 tributaries of the Jinsha River and Lancang River in Yunnan Province. Shi Jiayang designed, supervised the repair of three hydropower stations himself and proposed the plan of water resources development in Yunnan Province.

After the victory of the Anti-Japan War, Shi Jiayang returned to Tsinghua University with president Mei Yiqi to repair and restructure the campus. He also used the one-year vacation to investigate the large-scale hydropower station in the United States, the comprehensive utilization plan of the Tennessee Valley, and the cascade hydropower stations on the Columbia River, as well as learn from the regulation experience of the Mississippi River.

After the founding of the People's Republic of China, Tsinghua University added departments such as the Department of Hydraulic Engineering. Shi Jiayang served as the director of the academic research group on hydrology and water resources utilization in the water resources department. As the country was in urgent need of all kinds of specialized talents, the department of water conservancy opened a special concentration in hydrology. Shi Jiayang compiled several professional textbooks such as *Terrestrial Hydrology*, *Hydrological Forecasting*, and *River Regulation Project* on a tight 2-year period and taught these courses personally, which were welcomed by students. He paid attention to combining water resources planning problems in China into his class content to develop students with a good academic style that connects theories to realities.

In 1958, Shi Jiayang proposed the idea that reservoirs under construction should also assist with flood control, power generation, irrigation, and shipping. Thus, the course "The Study of Water Resources" should be adapted to "Comprehensive Utilization of Water Resources" to better serve China's water conservancy construction. In the early 1960s, Shi Jiayang still worked extremely hard with young teachers to investigate the Huai River regulation project, the Yangtze River flood control and levee project, hydropower stations at Xin'an River, Fuchun River, and the Guangxi Province Inland River Navigation Project. He collected a large number of first-hand data and prepared to write the textbook *Comprehensive Utilization of Water Resources*. The textbook was composed of five volumes with about 700,000 words. It was the first self-compiled textbook on China's comprehensive utilization of water resources.

As a teacher, Shi Jiayang focused on connecting theories to realities and developing teaching materials. According to the development of water conservancy construction at home and abroad, he constantly revised the textbook for improvement, strived for the education and teaching causes of engineering schools in China throughout his life, and achieved fruitful academic results. He actively conducted scientific research, carried out comprehensive analysis and argumentation on relevant topics of many water conservancy projects in China, and put forward many important suggestions on the development and planning of hydropower.

LI FUDU

Who Devoted His Life to the Yellow River

In the past, Li Bing and his son built Dujiangyan. Now, Li Yili and his nephew devoted themselves to the undertakings of water conservancy. It can be concluded that Li Fudu inherited the career from his uncle. Li Fudu was dedicated to regulating the Yellow River for his whole life. Even when he was almost blind due to the pressure on his optic nerve caused by thrombosis late in life, he was still concerned about regulating of the Yellow River. In a semi-blind state, he persisted in fumbling. He completed his last article, "The Radical Cure of Yellow River Regulation" before his death, which left a valuable legacy of river regulation for later generations.

LI FUDU (1903–1984), a native of Pucheng, Shaanxi Province, was an expert on issues on the Yellow River and a professor of hydraulic engineering. He once served as an engineer at Shaanxi Water Resources Bureau and a professor in the Department of Hydraulics at Henan University's School of Engineering.

Li Fudu

Li Fudu was born to a family of water regulation professionals. He left his hometown at a young age and followed his uncle, Mr. Li Yichang, to study in Xi'an, Nanjing, and Shanghai. Then he went to Germany to study hydraulics and returned to China with an excellent grade to commit to the development of water conservancy.

After Li Fudu returned to China, he was successively appointed as the Chief Engineer by Chongqing Yuchuan Road Bureau and Northeast China Rice Bureau. He followed his uncle Mr. Li Yichang and his teacher to survey the system of Huai River, formulated a dredging plan, and put great efforts into the planning of diverting Huai River. Later, Li Fudu was appointed as Chief Engineer and Chief of Project Affairs of North China Water Conservancy Commission. There, he actively practiced, carefully studied, and deeply understood the rivers in North China and completed writing the outline for the plan of North China Hydraulic Test Institute.

Li Fudu went back to China after finishing his study in Germany again. He presided over the design and construction of the "First Hydraulic Test Institute of China." He was appointed as the director to carry out experiments and research on the river regulation model of the river channels in the lower reaches of the Yellow River. When he was serving as the director of the design office of the Sichuan, he led the project's design and construction, which improved the irrigation conditions of the surrounding land. During his assignment as the Minister of Water Resources at Northwest Military and Political Commission, he investigated the Xinjiang Tianshan Reservoir Project in person, reviewed the water conservancy project plans of provinces in Northwest China, and actively led the construction of water conservancy projects. His efforts and achievements were lauded by the public.

With his knowledge, Li Fudu was eager to contribute to the development of China's water conservancy construction. But due to the limits of the past chaotic era, experiments and research he engaged in could not be carried out. After the founding of the People's Republic of China, Li Fudu devoted himself to the water conservancy construction of New China with great enthusiasm. He was appointed as both the chief director and director of academic affairs at Northwest Agriculture College. He also served as the director of the Yellow River Upper Reaches Project Division and the director of the Northwest Yellow River Project Bureau. He wrote many lecture notes, including "A General Introduction to River," "Hydrostatics," and "Water Circulation," and explored training methods for developing water conservancy talents.

The first hydraulic test laboratory in China

After Li Fudu served as the deputy director of the Yellow River Conservancy Commission of the Ministry of Water Resources, he devoted all his efforts to regulating the Yellow River. He dived into the study and investigation to understand the water and soil conservation, repair and prevention in the lower reaches, waterway regulation, and many other issues of the Yellow River. While controlling the Yellow River, Li Fudu personally presided over the research of Yellow River's water conservancy, put forward many important ideas on the radical cure of regulation and development of the Yellow River, and actively participated in several studies of the Yellow River. While regulating the Yellow River, Li Fudu took an active part in the academic research and practice of Yellow River's regulation. He wrote many works, such as *An Overview of Locations of Water and Soil Erosion Areas in the Yellow River Basin*, *The Crux of the Yellow River*, *The Regulation of the Yellow River Discharge*, *The Effect of the Mud Dam, Riverbed Evolution and Waterway Regulation of the Lower Reaches of Yellow River*, and *The Regulation of the Gully in the Water and Soil Erosion Areas in the Middle Reaches of the Yellow River*. Those books provided theoretical support and advanced the development of Yellow River regulation, making great contributions to water conservancy construction in the new China.

WANG HUAYUN

The First "River Officer" on the Yellow River

Wang Huayun once said, "If the Xiaolangdi Dam project doesn't launch, I will die with regret!" This has deeply expressed his unattachable feelings for the Xiaolangdi Dam project. As the saying goes, "As long as the Yellow River is calm, the world will be peaceful." The successful construction of the Xiaolangdi Dam Project was inseparable from the first "River Officer," who was devoted to the undertakings of regulating the Yellow River under the leadership of the Communist Party of China. He once led the workers and the people to repair the old levee at the lower reaches of the Yellow River with a gun in one hand and a shovel in the other. He proposed the idea of "no flood diversion" for decision-making, which enabled the Yellow River's flood to flow smoothly into the sea and safely protected people's lives and property. As he quoted in his 1955 work "A Report on the Flood Eradication and Water Resources Development of the Yellow River," "If I don't control the flood, how can I face all lives in the world?"

WANG HUAYUN (1908–1992) was born in Guantao County, Zhili Province (now Hebei Province). He was a member of the Communist Party of China and a modern Chinese hydraulic scientist. He participated in the anti-Japan movement to save China at an early age and joined the Communist Party in 1938. He was appointed as the director of the Yellow River Conservancy Commission of Hebei, Shandong, and Henan Provinces in 1946 and the director of the Yellow River Conservancy Commission of the Ministry of Water Resources in 1949. He had become the first "River Officer" of the People's Republic of China and devoted his whole life to the undertakings of Yellow River regulation.

Wang Huayun

"Take good care of all Yellow River related affairs." This is Comrade Mao Zedong's instruction to Wang Huayun, which he also regarded as his mission in life. Wang Huayun developed a series of ideas of river regulation, ranging from the initial "stick the Yellow River to where it is" (which means to not change the route of the Yellow River), to the later "eradicate the harm, benefit the water conservancy and comprehensively utilize the Yellow River," "widen the river to consolidate the dive," "intercept upper flow and drain the lower flow," and "store the water and retain the sediment," etc. These ideas resulted from Wang Huayun's diligent study, non-stop thinking, and broad investigations. Under the guidance of the series of ideas, Wang Huayun led the personnel of Yellow River water conservancy and built Sanmenxia Hydro-electric Complex Project as well as hydropower stations at Liujia Gorge, Yanguo Gorge, etc. In regard to "drain the lower flow," he carried out three times of levee reinforcement and overhaul projects after the founding of the People's Republic of China, which eliminated the accident potential of the levee, built projects for temporary flood storage and discharge, and significantly improved the flood control capacity of the lower reaches of the Yellow River. In July 1958, a flood occurred in Huayuankou, Zhengzhou Province, a town on the lower reaches of the Yellow River. It was the first largest flood on record ever since the field data existed. Premier Zhou Enlai led the flood control in person, and Wang Huayun was appointed as the commander-in-chief. In order to protect people's production and be responsible to the people, he studied and judged various situations and decisively proposed not to divert the flood but to overcome it by relying on dikes and the people instead. With the approval of Premier Zhou Enlai, the party, government, army, and people fought together and finally overcame the flood, ensured the safety of the dike, and avoided the major losses that could have been caused by flood diversion.

Thanks to the unremitting efforts of Wang Huayun for many years, the Xiaolangdi Hydropower Station Project eventually started in 1991. As one of China's two major world-renowned hydraulic projects at that time, the Xiaolangdi project was of great complexity and scale. It was one of the most challenging dam construction projects in the world's history. Its completion led to the improvement in the flood control capacity of the lower reaches of the Yellow River from 60 years per flood to 1000 years per flood. The area of agricultural irrigation greatly increased, which significantly relieved the cutoff in the Yellow River. The project brought tremendous comprehensive benefits at the beginning of its operation. It played an important role in guaranteeing the safety of life and property of the people who lived in the middle and lower reaches of the Yellow River, promoting economic and social development and protecting ecology and the environment.

In addition, Wang Huayun put forward a set of regulation policies on water and soil conservation, which advanced its development. He also actively advocated the construction of the South-to-North Water Diversion Project. As early as Comrade Mao Zedong's visit to the Yellow River in 1952, Wang Huayun proposed the idea of the South-North Water Diversion Project. Later, he organized teams and personally participated in the survey of water transfer routes many times, which furthered the development of the South-to-North Water Diversion Project.

Wang Huayun had been dedicated to the Yellow River regulation for 40 years. He is an important figure in the history of people's regulation of the Yellow River. He was also the first "River Officer" of the Communist Party of China and the first leader of the people's agency of Yellow River regulation. Because of his lifelong loyalty to the water conservancy undertakings, selfless dedication, and high degree of responsibility to the people, he became a true successor of Yu in people's hearts.

Xiaolangdi Hydropower Station Project

HUANG WENXI

Who Is Good at Studying and up for Challenges

Huang Wenxi was admitted to the program sponsored by Tsinghua University to study in the United States in 1933. He was awarded the Feitaofei Honorary Award for outstanding grades when obtaining his master's degree. He was also granted the exception to study for a doctor degree without an admission exam. He was awarded the Sigma Zeta Honor Award when he later graduated. At the time, he was praised in an exclusive newspaper article as "the most talented student in years at the University of Michigan with outstanding achievements in both structural and hydraulic studies." With such achievements, this young man cared deeply for his motherland and had devoted his whole life to the undertakings of Chinese water conservancy and geotechnical engineering.

HUANG WENXI (1909–2001), was born in Wujiang, Jiangsu Province. He was a member of the Communist Party of China and one of the major founders of China's soil mechanics and geotechnical engineering disciplines. He was an expert in hydraulic structure and geotechnical engineering. He was also a pioneer in the scientific research of hydraulics and hydropower in New China and an academician of the Chinese Academy of Sciences.

Huang Wenxi

Huang Wenxi graduated from the Civil Engineering Department of National Central University in 1929. After that, he graduated with a master's degree and then a doctorate degree from the University of Michigan. After he returned to China, he worked in Zhejiang Water Resources Bureau and Xi'an Northeast University. He first started a course in soil mechanics in China and founded the first geotechnical laboratory among domestic universities.

After the founding of the People's Republic of China, Huang Wenxi served as a professor in the Hydraulic Engineering Department of the Engineering School of Nanjing University. In 1952, after the adjustment of colleges and departments, he successively taught at Nanjing Institute of Technology and East China Engineering School of Water Resources. He became a professor at Hohai University from 1952 to 1956 and founded its first geotechnical engineering laboratory. He also served as the director of the Nanjing Hydraulic Laboratory of the Ministry of Water Resources, responsible for leading the work of the earliest and most large-scale hydraulic research institution established in China. He completed a lot of pioneering work for hydraulic development in New China.

Huang Wenxi actively planned and advanced the research work in new fields such as sediment, tidal wave, and structural materials. He undertook the experimental research tasks of regulation of Yellow River and Huai River and the hydropower projects in East China, which solved a lot of practical engineering problems. He organized the research and development of many hydraulic and geotechnical test instruments, led the compilation of test manuals and training of test technicians, and set up four classes for studying hydraulic tests. All the above made Nanjing Water Hydraulic Test Department the hydraulic research institution with the largest scale and highest level in China then. In 1955, Huang joined the Communist Party of China.

In 1956, Huang Wenxi was transferred to Tsinghua University and concurrently served as the Vice President of the Hydraulics Research Institute of the Ministry of Water Resources and the Director of the Geotechnical Research Institute. Following his leadership and efforts, the Hydraulic Research Institute established nine research offices and a complete technical logistics system, enabling it to undertake various major hydraulic scientific research projects, which developed a series of high-quality scientific research achievements and solved a large number of difficult problems in hydraulic projects.

Engineering Properties of Soil

Huang Wenxi studied rigorously. He was a fast learner with an agile way of thinking and rich experience. He participated in a large number of research and consulting projects for sluices, earth-rock dams, concrete dams, and foundations. He introduced and promoted many advanced technologies, such as seepage damage prevention using reverse filtration method and relief well, soft soil foundation reinforcement using sand-drained preloading method, sluices construction without pile foundation using the principle of compensated foundation, etc. Based on the extensive construction of water dumping dams and slurry-fall fill dams in China, he analyzed and tested the characteristics of dam fill, the estimation of dam pore water pressure, and construction practices from both theoretical and experimental perspectives. He has thus enriched and promoted dam construction technology with Chinese characteristics.

Huang Wenxi also made great achievements in the area of education. At the home front of the Anti-Japanese War, he diligently prepared lessons day and night, answered questions for students, and spared no effort to cultivate and promote young talents. Huang Wenxi has committed to hydraulic engineering education for more than half a century. Many of his students and assistants have become academicians, doctoral supervisors, famous experts, and scholars.

WANG HETING

Who Deeply Cared about Xinjiang's Water Conservancy

In 1944, Wang Heting made a big life decision. He decided to go to Xinjiang! At that time, Xinjiang was still ruled by warlords under a turbulent situation. He was going there at the risk of life. He had to withdraw from Xinjiang only one year after his first visit and then went there again in 1946. He carried out preliminary project construction tasks under difficult conditions. He always remembered that he was born into a farmer's family and was dedicated to following Mr.Li Yichang's mission to free the farmers in Northwest China from irrigation and water conservancy issues. He once said that liberation brought a bright future and opportunities for Xinjiang and its water conservancy undertakings. Since then, Xinjiang had become the place that Wang Heting deeply cared about. The construction and development of water conservancy in Xinjiang also became the cause that Wang Heting fought for and dedicated to his whole life until the very last moment.

WANG HETING (1910–1996), a native of Jiangyin, Jiangsu Province, was an expert in irrigation and a pioneer of modern water conservancy undertakings in Xinjiang. He was a former member of the China Association for Science and Technology, the vice chairman, and the honorary chairman of Xinjiang Uygur Autonomous Region's Association for Science and Technology. He also served as the director of the China Hydraulic Engineering Society and vice chairman of the China Environmental Hydraulics Society.

Wang Heting

In 1933, Wang Heting graduated from the Civil Engineering Department of the National Central University and then went to work at the Huai River Diversion Committee. At a young age, he undertook the design of the Huaiyin Navigation Lock, the first modern navigation lock in the Huaiyin-Yangzhou reach of the Grand Canal. He also actively participated in the construction for self-improvement, even giving up the opportunity to study abroad.

After the People's Republic of China was founded, following General Wang Zhen's leadership, Wang Heting and several water conservancy technical officials of the Water Resources Bureau began to map out Xinjiang's water conservancy blueprint. He served as the general manager of irrigation planning and development of the army reclamation farm. He cooperated with the military forces on both the north and south side of Tian Shan to build permanent hydraulic projects with considerable scale. Farms were opened up one after another while reservoirs and irrigation areas were built one after each. Wang Heting advocated the use of "cement substitution" and soil and stone materials collected from local earth. He also insisted on the construction of a diversion-type "plain reservoir," which has become a major unique feature of the water conservancy development in Xinjiang.

Within just four years after the founding of the People's Republic of China, Wang Heting led the completion of the Hongyanchi and Peace Canal projects. The construction of reservoir projects including Bayi, Mengjin, Daquangou, Mushroom Lake, and more than ten major key hydraulic projects such as Victory Canal, Jiefang Canal No. 1, Jiefang Canal No. 2, Hongxing Canal No. 2, Manas River West Bank Channel, and East Bank Channel was almost done too.

Victory Canal

It was Wang Heting's long-cherished wish to contribute his part to Xinjiang's water conservancy undertakings. His footprints were all over Xinjiang Province. After the Third Plenary Session of the 11th Central Committee of the Communist Party of China (CPC) was held, Wang Heting, despite being over 70 years old, still worked tirelessly for different hydraulic construction sites, technical review meetings, and academic seminars. He strived to develop water conservancy in Xinjiang till the very last moment of his life.

Wang Heting's selfless and patriotic spirit was recognized by Qian Zhengying, the former Vice Chairman of the National Committee of the Chinese People's Political Consultative Conference and the former Minister of Water Resources. He said, "Wang Heting is a groundbreaker for Xinjiang's water conservancy undertakings during the New China era." His working style of upholding the truth, seeking truth from facts, and seeing the big picture was also unanimously praised by the public, calling him the "True Expert in Technology."

LIU GUANGWEN

Who Had a Bright Hydrologic Career

Liu Guangwen was benevolent, drawing a clear line between his public and private life. He lived a frugal life and always treated people with tolerance and kindness. He had a small and simple home without any decent furniture or appliances. The bedroom was also used as a living room, in which a row of old bookcases of about one person's height was placed next to the wall, filled with professional books and literature published at home and abroad. There were also books stacked on the floor beside the bed due to the limited space of the bookcases. Liu Guangwen always had a frugal lifestyle and wore a few old clothes for decades. What was unknown is that he barely desired wealth and thus helped others using his own righteously his entire life. When the Anti-Japanese War had just ended, he went to Tianjin to sell a luxurious family estate to support several friends in difficult financial situations. The money left was not even enough for him to buy a pair of dentures.

LIU GUANGWEN (1910–1998), who styled himself Boru, was born in Hangzhou, Zhejiang Province. He was a hydrologist, educator, and founder of the higher education of hydrology in New China. He was a pioneer of hydrology, a professor, and a doctoral supervisor at Hohai University.

Liu Guangwen graduated from Tsinghua University in 1933. A few years after graduation, he went to Iowa State University in the United States to study, obtained a master's degree in hydraulic engineering, and then went to the Technical University of Berlin in Germany for postgraduate studies in hydraulic engineering and applied mathematics. He later returned to China in 1938.

Liu Guangwen

Since 1939, Liu Guangwen had been a professor at Guangxi University, Chongqing University, and several other universities. He also served as a Commissioner in Chongqing Central Hydraulic Experiment Office, where he researched Yellow River's regulation. After the victory of the Anti-Japanese War, he served as a professor at both Shanghai Jiaotong University and Fudan University.

In 1952, adjustments to colleges and departments were made to higher education in China. All hydraulic academic resources from Nanjing University, Shanghai Jiaotong University, Zhejiang University, Tongji University, and other universities in East China were incorporated and relocated to East China Water Conservancy College (now Hohai University) in Nanjing. Liu Guangwen participated in the process and was relocated from Shanghai to Nanjing. He served as the full professor and the director of the Hydrology School in East China Water Conservancy College and established China's first hydrology and terrestrial hydrology majors. He also served as the dean and honorary director of the school for a long time. He spared no efforts to train highly skilled hydrologic talents for the development of New China. He drafted teaching plans and syllabuses, hired teachers, compiled textbooks, and taught courses.

He led teachers to participate in scientific research and production activities, translated and published foreign hydrology monographs. He also instructed the first batch of graduate students in hydrology major collaboratively with Soviet experts. Led by Liu Guangwen, the hydrology discipline became the only key hydrologic discipline in China for a long time. It passed the national poll of key hydrologic disciplines with full votes in 2001. It attracted many famous foreign scholars to come for lecturing and held advanced programs of international hydrology studies entrusted by the International Hydrographic Organization many times.

Since the 1950s, Liu Guangwen has presided over the design flood research of the Three Gorges Project. Under his leadership, the scientific research team of the Three Gorges Project, together with the Yangtze River Basin Planning Office (now the Yangtze River Conservancy Commission) and the Chinese Academy of Sciences, put forward the approach of combining weather patterns to speculate the maximum precipitation and the maximum flood of the Three Gorges. It not only provided a reference for the feasibility study and preliminary design of the Three Gorges Project but also marked the first design flood of a hydrologic and meteorological estimation project in China. Liu Guangwen also served as a consultant for the hydrologic expert group of the Three Gorges Project and participated in the review of relevant results. He was also involved in demonstrating and reviewing the design flood of many large and medium-sized reservoirs in China. He was responsible for founding the Nanjing Hydrologic Research Office of the Chinese Academy of Sciences. He also obtained many important achievements in research and cultivated a large number of high-quality professionals.

Liu Guangwen was the main editor of *Hydrologic Analysis and Calculation*, a hydrologic textbook that has influenced several generations of students. It was a class textbook for the hydrologic major in China, which puts forward the basic theory and method of hydrologic analysis and calculation. He participated in writing and compiling a variety of books and academic materials, including but not limited to *English to Chinese Hydrologic Vocabulary*, *Introduction to Hydrologic Probability and Statistics*, *Common charts in Hydrologic Statistics*, *Applied Mathematics*, *Hydrologic Statistics and Approximate Calculation*, "Review of Hydrologic Frequency Calculation," "Parameter Estimation of Pearson Type III Distribution," "Interpolation Extension of Hydrologic Series," "Introduction to Hydrologic Calculation Error," all of which made important contributions to the development of hydrology in China.

LIN YISHAN

The Patriotic Expert Who Was Called "The King of Yangtze River"

In 1931, during the Mukden Incident, Lin Yishan devoted himself to the Anti-Japanese National Salvation Movement that was in full swing. In 1942, together with the commanders of the Eighth Route Army, he broke through the cruel encirclement of Jiaodong Peninsula, which was led by Niyuki Okamura, the commander-in-chief of Japan's North China dispatched army, for four times. After the victory of the Anti-Japanese War in 1945, he was ordered to advance into Northeast China, where he established the revolutionary base area of southern Liaoning and served as the Secretary of the Provincial Party Committee and Political Commissar of the Military Region in southern Liaoning. He organized a patriotic student movement and participated in the Anti-Japanese War. He was an experienced resolutioner during China's War of Liberation as well as the founder of the Yangtze River Conservancy Commission. He was a hydraulic expert appreciated by Chairman Mao and Premier Zhou as well as the famous "The King of the Yangtze River" at home and abroad. He lived a simple life and was fully dedicated to water conservancy. He even declined promotion opportunities six times.

LIN YISHAN (1911–2007) was born in Wendeng, Shandong Province. He was an outstanding member of the Communist Party of China and an experienced communist fighter. While still a middle school student, he actively participated in the Anti-Japanese National Salvation Movement. In 1934, he participated in the revolutionary work and was admitted to Beiping Normal University the next year. In 1936, he joined the Communist Party of China, became a famous hydraulic expert in modern China, and was called "The King of the Yangtze River" by Chairman Mao.

When the People's Republic of China was just founded, Lin Yishan devoted himself to the great cause of Yangtze River regulation following the order of the Party. In February 1950, he participated in founding the "Yangtze River Conservancy Commission." He started dedicating himself

Lin Yishan

to researching and exploring China's water conservancy development and the comprehensive regulation and development of the Yangtze River basin. Lin Yishan proposed a "high ladder" strategy for the Three Gorges Project, which was gradually deployed and implemented. In 1950, he led the construction of the Jingjiang River Flood Diversion Project. As a starting point, the project took only 75 days to finish under his leadership, which was a miracle in the construction history of hydraulic projects in China. In 1958, he proposed building a land and water conservancy project to gain experience and provide a scientific basis for constructing the Three Gorges Project. He led the construction of the painstaking project Danjiangkou Reservoir, which was not only an important flood control project for the Han River but also a water source project for the South-North Water Diversion Project. It became a model of China's Five

Benefits All in One[1] water conservancy projects. He also trained a large number of technical talents for the future construction of the Three Gorges Project and led the construction of the Gezhouba Project as a preparation for the Three Gorges Project.

Gezhouba Dam Junction

Lin Yishan solved the navigation problem of the reaches below the Three Gorges Dam and recovered the hydraulic head. He studied the scheme of "cofferdam hydropower" and "phased development" and summarized the policy of replacing "relocation" with "relocation and settlement." He also wrote the paper "Problems of Reservoir's Long-term Use," which discussed how to extend the Three Gorges Reservoir's service life indefinitely.

In 1972, Lin Yishan was diagnosed with cancer. During his hospitalization, he was appointed as the director of the technical committee of the Gezhouba Project to solve the urgent issues the project faced. Based on

Danjiangkou Dam

the River Dialectics and River Regime Planning theories, he took several actions, including excavating Gezhouba, a small island in the river center,[2] and deploying the junction with a "one body and two wings" structure, etc. He saved the Gezhouba Dam Project from trouble and eventually developed it into a world-renowned high-quality project.

Lin Yishan proposed the "South-North Water Diversion Project Plan" for West China, which found the solution to the water shortage in Northwest China as well as the Gobi Desert of Xinjiang. He also proposed the river regulation strategy of "preserving the water and sand of the Yellow River as precious resources." He carried out the experiment of "releasing silt to revolutionize rice planting" himself in the 1960s, which soon became successful and popular among the public.

Lin Yishan's contribution to China's water conservancy undertakings and Yangtze River regulation and his spirit of living a simple life and bold exploration have become a monument to Yangtze River's history.

---

1. TN: Five benefits include benefits in flood protection, power generation, navigation, irrigation and aquatic products.
2. TN: The Gezhouba Dam project was named after this island.

XU ZHILUN

Who Had the Patriotic Spirit to Save China through Education

When Xu Zhilun studied at the Massachusetts Institute of Technology, he once lived with Qian Xuesen. They encouraged each other and studied diligently, hoping to pay back to their motherland in the future. Xu Zhilun started his educational career at Zhejiang University to save the nation through education. Being exposed to the danger of the anti-Japanese war, Zhejiang University moved to west China. As a young teacher, with firm actions and belief, Xu Zhilun wrote, "A sharp sword can only be made by grinding," as a wonderful opening line for his life.

Xu Zhilun (1911–1999) was born in Jiangdu, Jiangsu Province. He was a member of the Communist Party of China, an expert in engineering mechanics, an educator in mechanics, and an academician of the Chinese Academy of Sciences.

Xu Zhilun was born into an intellectual family and studied hard from a young age. In 1934, he graduated from the Department of Civil Engineering of Tsinghua University. In 1936, he graduated with a master's degree in civil engineering from the Massachusetts Institute of Technology, following another master's degree in engineering science from Harvard University in 1937. At that time, China suffered from the difficult era of national calamity being ravaged by the Japanese invaders. He declined the offer with attractive benefits from his two advisors to stay at MIT. He also gave up the opportunity to study for a doctor's degree and returned

Xu Zhilun

to China in 1937 with a strong desire to save the nation. He then began his educational career by teaching at Zhejiang University.

From 1937 to 1943, Xu Zhilun taught more than ten courses at Zhejiang University, such as *Applied Mechanics*, *Material Mechanics*, and *Structural Mechanics*. To gain more practical experience in engineering, he left Zhejiang University in 1943 and returned to educational institutes in 1944. He first served as a professor at National Central University, then transferred to Shanghai Jiaotong University after the victory of the Anti-Japanese War. In 1948, he also served as the director of the School of Water Resources. Through the long-term teaching practice, his teaching level continued to improve with increasingly abundant instruction skills.

After the founding of the People's Republic of China, due to the urgent need to develop water conservancy, the Party and the state established East China Water Conservancy College (now Hohai University) in 1952. Xu Zhilun followed the assignment and moved to Nanjing to participate in the establishment of the first water conservancy school in New China. He first served as a professor and the director of the academic research office of engineering mechanics. He concurrently served as the dean in 1954 and then the vice president in 1956. While undertaking administrative work, he insisted on teaching. He compiled and published more than ten kinds of textbooks, including *Engineering Mechanics Course, Elasticity Theory, and Elasticity Mechanics* (Volume I and II), which were widely adopted in China. The first edition of *Elasticity Mechanics* (Volume I and II) won the annual National Book Award for Scientific and Technological Book from 1977 to 1981. The second edition won the Outstanding Prize of the

Elasticity (Volume I and II)

National Textbook Award in 1988. Since 1978, he has served as the Deputy Director of the National Committee for Compilation and Review of Engineering Mechanics Higher Education Textbooks, making great contributions to the development of higher education mechanics textbooks.

In the 1960s, following the need for national large-scale water conservancy development, Xu Zhilun carried out research on the calculation of hydraulic structures using the principle of elastic mechanics, the results of which led to the publication of papers such as *Thermal Stress of Foundation Beam* and *Foundation Beam of Elastic Foundation with Medium-thickness*. His research on the mechanics of foundation beams and foundation plates had always been the top place globally. He guided young teachers to study how to calculate the internal force of foundation beams under overload and converted the research results into tables for application. He then successively formulated calculation tables of a foundation beam on the Winkler foundation and foundation with a medium thickness. These tables remained as important data for designers to date. By the end of the 1960s, he took part in the design of Chu River's sluice gate, where he first applied elasticity mechanics to design a new type of double-curvature shallow shell gate which was economical and easier to construct.

In the early 1970s, Xu Zhilun actively searched and translated foreign literature and found the Finite Element Method, a method to solve complex elastic mechanics problems using the electronic computer. In 1974, he published China's first monograph on the finite element method, *Finite Element Method to Elastic Mechanics Problems*, which was groundbreaking and foundation-setting for promoting the finite element method.

With his patriotic spirit to save and rejuvenate China through education, Xu Zhilun made great contributions to the education and scientific research of mechanics, hydraulics, and hydropower engineering in China.

ZHANG GUANGDOU

Who Deeply Cared about His Motherland and Its Landscape

When the nationwide Anti-Japanese War broke out in 1937, Zhang Guangdou had just obtained a master's degree in the United States and received a scholarship to continue his doctoral study at Harvard University. But the war made it impossible for him to focus on studying anymore. He thought, "What's the point of my study if my country is gone?" Driven by the spirit of "All men share the responsibility for the rise and fall of the country," he resolutely decided to give up the attractive opportunity to continue his study and return to China to participate in the movement of resisting Japan to save the nation. He even brought his newlywed to the construction site in a remote poor valley in Sichuan all the way from the prosperous Shanghai regardless of the potential hardship of life. There, he built a batch of small hydropower stations, which provided electricity for military production in Changshou and Wan County and supported the War of Resistance.

ZHANG GUANGDOU (1912–2013) was born in Changshu, Jiangsu Province. He was a member of the Communist Party of China and an expert and educator in hydraulic and hydropower engineering. He was one of the main pioneers of China's water conservancy undertakings and academicians of the Chinese Academy of Sciences and the Chinese Academy of Engineering. He was also a foreign academician of the National Academy of Engineering of Mexico. He served as the vice president of Tsinghua University and the president of the China Institute of Water Resources and Hydropower Research of the Department of Water Resources of the Chinese Academy of Sciences.

Zhang Guangdou

Zhang Guangdou graduated from Shanghai Jiaotong University in 1934 with a bachelor's degree. He obtained a master's degree in civil engineering from the University of California in 1936 and another master's degree in engineering mechanics from Harvard University in 1937. He was also offered a full scholarship to study for doctoral studies, but he resolutely gave up this opportunity.

After returning to China in 1937, Zhang Guangdou immediately devoted himself to the development of water conservancy in China. From 1937 to 1942, he was responsible for the design of Taohuaxi, Xiaqingyuan Cave, Xiannv Cave, and other hydropower stations, which were the first batch of hydropower stations completely self-designed and constructed by the Chinese. In 1951, he was in charge of the layout and structural design of the head sluice of the People's Victory Canal as part of the project to divert the Yellow River to the Wei River. He succeeded in diverting water from the lower reaches of the Yellow River by breaking the embankment, which paved an effective path for irrigating the farmlands in the lower reaches by diverting the Yellow River. In 1958, he was appointed the Chief Engineer to lead the design of Miyun Reservoir, the largest reservoir in North China. He innovatively adopted revolutionary technologies such as concrete cut-off walls with deep overburden layers, thin clay inclined walls of high earth-rock fill dam, and gallery diversion under earth dam for the first time. Miyun Reservoir was able to relieve flood within a year and was completed in two years, a speed that is rarely seen in the history of global hydraulic engineering. Zhang Guangdou also participated in the design and consultation of projects, including the People's Victory Canal, Jingjiang Flood Diversion Project, Danjiangkou Project, Sanmenxia

Miyun Reservoir

Project, Gezhouba Project, Ertan Hydroelectric Station, Xiaolangdi Project, and Three Gorges Project. He played an important role in solving complicated technical engineering problems and was thus being applauded as the Li Bing[1] in the modern era.

In the 1950s, Zhang Guangdou participated in formulating the development plan of the national science and technology development vision. During the formulation process, he provided suggestions with a scientific and practical attitude, which led to its adoption and approval. He attached great importance to production practice and fundamental hydraulic research. In 1955, he established a hydraulic structures laboratory and carried out structural model tests in China, such as the Liuxihe arch dam, Xianghongdian arch dam, etc. The tests solved several structural problems and gained the laboratory gained a great reputation.

Zhang Guangdou had always been paying great attention to his teaching practice. He taught lectures at Tsinghua University for more than 50 years. He was barely absent from the podium and dedicatedly educating the students as well as writing textbooks. Among his students are academicians of China's two academies, national top design masters, and many other senior engineers and professors. Many of them have made outstanding contributions to the cause of water conservancy and hydropower development in China while becoming its pillars.

Zhang Guangdou pursued the life philosophy to "patriotically dedicate," the construction principle to "rigorously practice," and the academic spirit to "diligently achieve" throughout his entire life. He was not only a conscientious and responsible person but also someone who dared to innovate and did things that had not been done before. He has contributed to China's water conservancy, hydropower development, and education for more than 70 years. He was an extraordinary pioneer of China's water conservancy and hydropower development and made outstanding contributions.

---

1. TN: Li Bing is Chinese hydraulic expert in the ancient Warring of the States ear who was revered for his work on the Dujiangyan Water Control Project.

YAN KAI

Who Gained Outstanding Achievements in Both Teaching and Research

Yan Kai focused on his work with full attention. He deeply cherished his time and honestly served the government. He never had any special requirements for basic necessities. Every time he went to investigate some provinces and cities, he would ask to reach an agreement with the local reception team, which is "No Guest Meal," "No Gifting," and "No Large-scale Preparation." Once, Yan Kai went to somewhere in Jiangsu Province to investigate the location of a port and offered great advice for the port construction, for which the port manager would like to pay compensation. Yan Kai resolutely declined. Later the manager came to Yan Kai's office at Hohai University, offering compensation again but was asked by Yan Kai to leave.

YAN KAI (1912–2006) was born in Minhou, Fujian Province. He was a member of the Communist Party of China and a hydraulic and coastal engineering scientist. He was an academician of the Chinese Academy of Sciences and Chinese Academy of Engineering and a foreign academician of the Mexican Academy of Sciences. He has served as Honorary President and doctoral advisor at Hohai University and Honorary President of Nanjing Hydraulic Research Institute of the Ministry of Water Resources and Ministry of Transportation. He was also the Honorary President of China Hydraulic Engineering Society and China Society for Oceanography.

Yan Kai

In 1933, Yan Kai graduated from the Tangshan Engineering College of Northern Jiaotong University. In 1935, he was qualified to study in the Netherlands with outstanding grades. He obtained a civil engineer degree from the Delft University of Technology in the Netherlands with excellent performance and achievements. After he returned to China, he first worked at the National Central University and then the Yellow River Conservancy Commission. However, even with great enthusiasm to serve China, he was unable to bring practical changes to the rivers due to the incompetence and corruption of the Kuomintang government.

In 1952, Yan Kai served as the Vice-Chairman of the founding committee of East China Water Conservancy College (now Hohai University) while being a professor there. He later became the vice-chairman and the president of the school too. He laid a solid foundation for the future development of this famous Chinese hydraulic higher education institution with his hard work, intelligence, and courage. In 1956, Yan Kai joined the Communist Party of China. Under the guidance of the Party, he created a new academic style of "Be Diligent and Simple," "Be Practical," "Be Strict on Oneself," and "Dare to Explore," which was later designated as the motto of Hohai University. He also concurrently served as the director of the Jiangsu Department of Water Resources and the director of Nanjing Hydraulic Research Institute, making great contributions to the development of Jiangsu's water conservancy undertakings.

As a pioneer, Yan Kai witnessed the kick-off and development of seaport construction and coastal engineering in New China. In 1951, he was appointed as a member of the Port Construction Committee of Tanggu Xingang Port (later renamed Tianjin Port.) He presided over the "Siltation of Tianjin Port" research project and

The finger-pier of the Port of Tianjin

initiated research on the muddy coast of China. He contributed to solving the serious siltation of Tianjin Port and building the deepwater port. He guided the comprehensive investigation and research on the national coastal zone resources. He also edited *A Comprehensive Investigation Report on China's Coastal Zone and Beaches Resources*, which provided scientific reasonings for developing and utilizing of China's coastal zone resources. The report won the first prize in the State Science and Technology Advancement Award in 1992. Yan Kai also made important achievements in the research on the interaction mechanism between wind waves and seawalls, as well as the sediment movement of coastal engineering. He was also the chief editor of *China Coastal Engineering* and won the Outstanding Prize for Excellent Academic Publications of Chinese Universities in 1995. His practice and research laid a solid foundation for the establishment of coastal dynamics and coastal dynamic geomorphology. He was also responsible for the research of regulation on the Yangtze River Estuary and Pearl River Delta for a long time while serving as the technical consultant for many major projects such as the Gezhouba Dam and the Three Gorges Project in the Yangtze River.

In 1996, Yan Kai won the first Engineering Science and Technology Award. He also won the Liang Heli Science and Technology Advancement Award later in 1997 and the Merit Award by China Hydraulic Engineering Society in 2001. Yan Kai held an extremely high status in the international academic society and groups. He has served as the Chairman of the Chinese Committee of the International Commission on Large Dams, the Chairman of the Intergovernmental Council of UNESCO's International Hydrologic Programme as well as the Chairman of its Chinese Committee. In 1995, he was awarded an honorary membership by the International Association for Hydro-Environment Engineering and Research. His achievements have earned China water conservancy a global reputation.

GU DEZHEN

The Founder of Engineering Geology

Gu Dezhen has always been a fan of Chairman Mao's poems, and he has been particularly looking forward to the scene "To hold back Wushan's clouds and rain, till a smooth lake rises in the narrow gorges" as depicted in "Swimming: To the Tune of Shui Tiao Keh Tou." On the day of the success of the river closure project of the Gezhouba Dam Project, he chanted the line from Chairman Mao's poem in his heart. He decided to name his newborn grandson "Guping Lake" to commemorate this important moment. He once wrote, "Spring follows winter to come, nature of the motherland becomes revitalized; my clothes are full of sweat climbing mountains and crossing rivers, but I feel calm when reflecting on myself."

GU DEZHEN (1914–1982) was from Mi County (now Xinmi City), Henan Province. He was a member of the Communist Party of China (CPC) and a member of the Chinese Academy of Sciences (CAS). He was a pioneer and founder of China's engineering geology and hydrogeology academia.

In 1936, Gu Dezhen was admitted to the School of Geology of Peking University. After the outbreak of the Anti-Japanese War, he suspended school to recuperate at home and actively participated in anti-Japanese propaganda activities in his hometown. He later went to the National Southwestern Associated

Gu Dezhen (second from the left) at work

University to study. After graduation, Gu Dezhen started working at the Sichuan Geological Engineering Survey Institute. He then worked as an assistant and assistant researcher in the Nanjing Center of China Geological Survey following Mr. Li Siguang.

After the founding of the People's Republic of China, the State began to carry out comprehensive regulation of the Huai River. In response to the national need for engineering geological talents, Gu Dezhen embarked on the road of engineering geological research and practice.

In 1951, Gu Dezhen served as the head of the geological team of Huai River regulation of the China Geological Project Steering Committee and conducted a series of engineering geological surveys for dam sites of the Huai River regulation projects. He deep dived into Foziling, Xianghongdian, Mozitan, Meishan, and other construction sites of Huai River regulation project, where he accumulated experience for the study and solution of engineering geological issues of hydraulic projects. He summarized "lithology, structure, and groundwater" as the three key engineering geology points. Under his leadership, the geological team regulating the Huai River carried out surveys on the engineering geology of ten reservoirs and their dams. His team compiled more than ten survey reports in total, providing scientific reasoning for the site selection, design and foundation treatment of dam area, dam site, and dam line.

In 1954, a catastrophic flood occurred in the Yangtze River basin, which led to the formulation of the Yangtze River basin planning and the development of Yangtze River's Three Gorges hydraulic project plan. Gu Dezhen served as the deputy chief engineer of the Yangtze River Basin Planning Office, then concurrently the chief engineer of the Three Gorges geological team of the Ministry of Geology, and the vice head of the Three Gorges engineering geological group of the State Scientific and Technological Commission in 1957. He participated in the appraisal of the engineering geology of the Three Gorges Sandouping and Danjiang Reservoir and the geological demonstration and evaluation of Min River Ziping Dam. In early 1956, Gu Dezhen and Hou Defeng wrote *The Engineering Geological Report on the Yangtze River Water Control Project by Sino-Soviet Geological Experts*. Gu Dezhen was appointed as the Chief Engineer of the geological survey team of the Three Gorges Project and carried out a series of tasks, including the investigation of regional geological and hydrogeological engineering geological conditions, the engineering geological survey of several proposed dam sites, and the study of reservoir leakage, which laid the foundation for the geological demonstration and evaluation of the construction of Three Gorges Project and the selection of the dam site.

From 1959 to 1961, Gu Dezhen presided over the geological survey of the South-North Water Diversion Project. From 1963 to 1965, he led the task of summarizing the engineering geology of hydraulic projects, which was the first time China systematically summarized engineering geology based on practice. It played an important role in promoting the development of engineering geology.

During his geological career, Gu Dezhen served as the leader of the engineering geology team of the Ministry of Geology, the leader of the engineering geology team of Wuhan Yangtze River Bridge, the chief geological engineer of the Yangtze River Basin Planning Office, the vice director of the Institute of Hydrogeology and Engineering Geology of the Academy of Geological Sciences, the director of the Hydrogeology and Engineering Geology Research Office of the Institute of Geology of the Chinese Academy of Sciences, and the first chairman of the Engineering Geology Professional Committee of the Geological Society of China. He has participated in many major national projects, including Huai River Regulation Project, Three Gorges Project, Gezhouba Project, Railway Construction in Southwest China, Ertanshui Hydropower Project, etc. During the construction of the Ertan Hydropower Station, he organized a scientific research team of more than 100 members to carry out the preliminary feasibility study for this important project.

In regard to theoretical research, Gu Dezhen was the pioneer and founder of "engineering rock geomechanics," which was an innovative branch of the geomechanics discipline with Chinese characteristics. He put forward the famous conclusion "rock mass structure controls rock mass stability," which advanced the development of China's engineering geology research and became a milestone in China's engineering geology discipline. Gu Dezhen won three Outstanding Prizes of the National Award for Natural Sciences with "The New Technology of Nanjing Yangtze River Bridge," "Gezhouba Project and its Hydroelectric Unit Installation," and "The Construction of Chengdu-Kunming Railway."

ZHU XIANMO

Who Cleaned the Yellow River's Water by Sediment Regulation with Deep Knowledge in Soil

Putting the country's needs first, Zhu Xianmo abandoned his superior living conditions in Nanjing and moved with his entire family to Yangling, a remote town in Wugong County, Shaanxi Province, in 1959, and settled there since. In order to find an effective way to control soil erosion in the Loess Plateau, he established a test site and invested large amounts of manpower and material resources in Ziwuling, which was called "a sample of the Loess Plateau." The place was extremely remote, with barren hills all around. It had limited accessibility with the very difficult living condition. Despite the harsh conditions, Zhu led the staff to conduct ongoing research.

ZHU XIANMO (1915–2017) was from Chongming, Jiangsu (now part of Shanghai). He was a member of the Communist Party of China, an expert in soil science and water and soil conservation, and an academician of the Chinese Academy of Sciences. He was also a researcher and doctoral advisor at the Institute of Soil and Water Conservation, Chinese Academy of Sciences & Ministry of Water Resources (Institute of Soil and Water Conservation of Northwest A&F University). He was once the first deputy director of the Northwest Institute of Soil and Water Conservation of the Chinese Academy of Sciences

Zhu Xianmo

and the honorary director of the Institute of Soil and Water Conservation, Chinese Academy of Sciences & Ministry of Water Resources.

In 1940, after graduating from the School of Agricultural Chemistry of National Central University, Zhu Xianmo started working at Jiangxi Geological Survey Institute and then transferred to the soil research office of Chongqing Institute of Geological Survey. After the People's Republic of China was founded, he worked at Nanjing Institute of Soil Science, Chinese Academy of Sciences. In 1959, he was formally transferred to work at the Institute of Soil and Water Conservation, Chinese Academy of Sciences, and Ministry of Water Resources (formerly Northwest Biological Soil Research Institute).

Zhu Xianmo went to Tongliang County (now Tongliang District) of Sichuan Province with his instructor Mr. Hou Guangjiong while working in the Soil Research Office of the Central Geological Survey. He later went to Guizhou, Guangxi, Hunan, Jiangxi, and other places for investigation. During the seven years he spent in Jiangxi, he carried out in-depth investigation and research on Jiangxi Province's soil and red soil tests. He proposed a new perspective on the occurrence and distribution of red soil and believed that "imported soil" and "burned soil" were the most effective methods for improving red soil in Jiangxi Province.

Regulating the Yellow River and reducing its sediment concentration had always been Zhu Xianmo's greatest wish. In his opinion, the Yellow River was called the "Yellow River" mainly due to the soil erosion of the Loess Plateau in the middle and upper reaches of the Yellow River. In the early 1950s, he made four visits to the Loess Plateau in Northwest China. He walked through the gullies and ridges of the Loess Plateau, went to chat with farmers one by one, and learned wisdom from

The scenery of Yellow River

their experiences. For decades, Zhu Xianmo has walked those gullies and ridges more than 20 times. He also crossed the Kunlun Mountains three times and entered Xinjiang twice. After numerous on-site investigations, Zhu Xianmo refined his decades of research results into a "28-word strategy" for land reclamation on the Loess Plateau. The 28 words are as follows: All precipitation was infiltrated locally, rice grains were stored on the upper tableland, forest fruits were stored on the upper ditch, and grass irrigation was stored on the upper slope. This simple 28-word strategy had become the key reference for Yellow River's regulation and the scientific foundation for the Loess Plateau to get rid of poverty. During the era when the state started to regulate the Yellow River basin comprehensively, he participated in water and soil conservation projects and completed a significant of detailed and comprehensive works. In 1958, Zhu Xianmo participated in the investigation group of soil erosion in the Yangtze River basin. He deep dived into the Three Gorges project and put forward the strategy of "Drain the river safely, intercept and store the water by sections," which achieved great results in practice. In 1959, in order to support the construction of Northwest China, he resolutely gave up the superior living conditions of Nanjing. He went to work at the Northwest Institute of Biological Soil, Chinese Academy of Sciences.

Zhu Xianmo was the pioneer and founder of the soil and soil erosion discipline in the Loess Plateau of China. To realize his dream of "a clear Yellow River," he had silently committed to and made great contributions to the sediment control in the middle reaches of the Yellow River at the vast Loess Plateau for more than half a century.

QIAN LINGXI

The "Academician Bole" Who Was a Leading Expert in Mechanics

In 1978, When attending the National Science Convention, Qian Lingxi, who was over 60 years old, was so excited that he could not sleep at night. He wrote the following lines, "I devote myself to the science and education following the spirit of spring silkworms, afraid of wasting my youth elsewhere; I look forward to seeing China rise, but I would be even happier with its abundant talents." This poem expressed his passionate love for China as a mechanics scientist and educator. It shows his character of devotion to science and education with persistent pursuit. The poem also shows his high expectations for the young generation and willingness to support them for higher achievements.

QIAN LINGXI (1916–2009), born in Wuxi, Jiangsu Province, was a member of the Communist Party of China. He was an engineering mechanician and educator, a pioneer of structural optimization design of computational mechanics engineering in China, and an academician of the Chinese Academy of Sciences.

He graduated from Sino-French Institute in Engineering (now the University of Shanghai for Science and Technology) in 1936, then obtained the top engineer degree from the Free University of Brussels in Belgium in 1938. After returning to China, Qian Lingxi came to Kunming and was admitted by Xu-Kun Railway Bureau. Since 1941, he has worked at Sichuan-Yunnan Railway Company, Yunnan University, Bridge Design and Engineering Department of the Ministry of Transportation, and Zhejiang University at Zunyi.

Qian Lingxi

In 1950, he served as director of the Department of Civil Engineering of Zhejiang University. In 1952, he was invited by Dr. Qu Bochuan, Dean of Dalian Institute of Technology (now Dalian University of Technology), many times to teach at the school. There, he worked in several positions, including the director of the mathematical mechanic school, the director of the research department, the director of the Research Institute of Engineering Mechanics, and the president of the Dalian Institute of Technology. His students spread all over the world, several of which later became academicians, such as Qiu Dahong, Hu Haichang, Pan Jiazheng, and Zhong Wanxie, for which he was called "Academician Bole."

In the 1950s, Qian Lingxi participated in the demonstration and design practice of several critical national projects, including the Wuhan Yangtze River Bridge, the Three Gorges Project, and the Nanjing Yangtze River Bridge. In the early 1960s, China decided to build its own nuclear submarine. The research team led by Qian Lingxi studied the strength, opening and stability of the shell for the construction of nuclear submarine. He strongly proposed to list computational mechanics as one of the key directions for developing mechanics disciplines. His suggestion was adopted eventually, thus marking a new chapter for computational mechanics development nationwide.

After the founding of the People's Republic of China, the government invested greatly in building hydraulic projects, for which the large thin-shell arch dam type was very favorable. At the time, it was still difficult to apply thin shell theory in arch dam analysis. The test load method that was commonly used abroad was too complicated, and its results were difficult to judge. The independent arch method and crown cantilever method that were normally applied in small and medium-sized dams, though based on the clear hypothesis of the mechanics model, are too rough, ignoring too many factors. Qian Lingxi published an article in 1959 that included the torsion effect of arch dam shells in the crown cantilever method. The method could have more precise results with little increase in the calculation. Therefore, the method was then applied to different projects.

In 1951, he was invited by the Huai River Regulation Commission to the construction site of Foziling Dam to jointly study and formulate the project plan together with experts such as Mao Yisheng and Zhang Guangdou. In 1959, he attended the Three Gorges Project Planning Conference, where he proposed a new type of buttress dam, the trapezoidal dam. It's a kind of dam that falls between the traditional gravity dam and the massive-head buttress dam and can be used for building high dams. It is economical and easy to dissipate heat during construction with a relatively small floating uplift force at the dam bottom. As the side height of the dam cross section is of an isosceles trapezoid, there is no sudden change within the cross-section, which avoids the tensile stress that may be generated in the internal head of the cross-section of massive-head dams. The most outstanding advantage of the dam type is convenient construction. Concrete projects can adopt a large area of flat formwork, which is advantageous for mass concrete pouring. This dam type was used by the Shanghai Investigation and Design Institute of the Ministry of Water Resources for the construction of Hunan Town Hydropower Station on the Wuxijiang River in Zhejiang Province. The dam is 128 meters high and 440 meters long, with 22 buttresses. It's China's highest buttress dam and was completed in October 1979.

Qian Lingxi devoted all his life to scientific research and engineering mechanics education. He cultivated generations of civil engineers and made important contributions to China's engineering technology fields, such as hydraulics, bridge, and harbor.

ZHANG RUIJIN

The Founder of "Zhang Ruijin Formula"

In 1949, Zhang Ruijin joined the New Democracy Education Association, an underground society led by the Communist Party of China. He joined the Communist Party of China in 1950, becoming the first professor at Wuhan University and a party member since the founding of the People's Republic of China. He had been full of enthusiasm throughout his decades of hydraulic career. In his sixties, Zhang Ruijin often quoted Cao Cao's poem, "An old war-horse may be stabled, yet it still longed to gallop a thousand miles; And a noble-hearted man though advanced in years, never abandons his proud aspirations." After the Reform and Opening-up, Zhang Ruijin was suffering from Parkinsonism, but he still worked actively to offer advice and contribute his own strength to China's water conservancy undertakings in the new era.

ZHANG RUIJIN (1917–1998) was born in Badong, Hubei Province. He was a member of the Communist Party of China, a hydraulic expert, and an educator. He was also a professor and a doctoral advisor. He once served as the President and Honorary President of the Wuhan Institute of Hydraulic and Electric Engineering (now Wuhan University). In 1939, he graduated from the School of Civil Engineering of Wuhan University, went to the University of California to study hydraulics in 1945, and interned at the Bureau of Reclamation, which was famous for the construction of hydraulic projects.

Zhang Ruijin

Zhang Ruijin had been researching fundamental theories and practically applied engineering studies of sediment movement for a long time. He once put forward the "dynamic water conservancy plan," namely irrigation, power generation, flood control, and navigation. The plan was groundbreaking at that time. In the 1940s, he participated in the observation, survey, and research related to the regulation of the Yellow River. He obtained the scientific data to estimate an annual sediment yield of 1.5 billion tons. But with the frequent wars, he felt his expertise could not be fully utilized and returned to teach at his alma mater, Wuhan University.

In the early days after the People's Republic of China was founded, the development of water conservancy was urgently needed. Zhang Ruijin went to the frontier of construction and made a series of theoretical achievements in sediment incipient, sedimentation, and sediment carrying capacity in academic research. The formula in these theoretical results was derived from a large number of measurements and experimental research by him and thus was called the "Zhang Ruijin Formula." This formula was widely applied and won the National Science Conference Award in 1978. In the 1960s, he began to study the movement of hyper-concentrated flow by using a large amount of first-hand data from the Yellow River survey in his early years.

In the 1970s, Zhang Ruijin and other scholars actively advised "A Radical Cure for the Yellow River" many times, which advanced the process of the national deployment of comprehensive regulation of the Yellow River. He participated in the design of the Gezhouba Project and the study of its sediment issues. Together with the team, he proposed the scheme of "static water for navigation, flowing water for sand sluicing, and machinery for dredging," which solved the sedimentation issue of the approaching channel of Gezhouba Navigation Lock. The scheme also contributed to the river regime planning of the Gezhouba Project, providing valuable experience for solving the sediment problem of the Three Gorges Project. In the early 1980s, Zhang Ruijin served as the Head of the Sediment Research Coordination Group of the Three Gorges Project and conducted a long-term demonstration of the sediment issues of the project, which paved the way for future research and solution. The efforts of Zhang Ruijin and other sediment research experts from the older generation enabled China to transform from a country with poor sediment solutions to a country experienced in sediment control.

River Sediment Dynamics

Zhang Ruijin successively served as vice provost of Wuhan University, vice dean of the School of Engineering, and the dean of the School of Water Resources. In the 1950s, he participated in founding the Wuhan Institute of Hydraulic and Electric Engineering and initiated the one and only undergraduate major in river sediment and river regulation engineering in the world at that time. He successively served as the Vice President, President, and Honorary President of the Wuhan Institute of Hydraulic and Electric Engineering, where he diligently educated talents and led scientific research to overcome key obstacles. He cultivated a large number of senior professionals and business backbone for China's water conservancy and electricity industry. While leading the school, he also undertook heavy tasks in teaching and compiling teaching material. He played an important role in maintaining the leading position in the teaching and research of the river sediment and river management engineering major globally. He was the editor-in-chief for publications including *Hydraulics*, *River Dynamics*, and *River Sediment Dynamics*, co-authored *Sediment Research in China*, and participated in compiling *River Sediment Engineering*. Among all his works, *River Sediment Dynamics* won the first prize in the Textbook Excellence Award of the Ministry of Water Resources, and *River Sediment Engineering* won the National Textbook Excellence Award.

LI E'DING

Who Surveyed Rivers and Devoted to Hydropower

In the autumn of 1981, a horrifying fight to control the flood and save the risk happened at the Longyangxia Hydropower Station at the Yellow River during its construction. At the time, Li E'ding suffered from coronary heart disease and diabetes and had been working only for half day in Beijing. At this critical moment, he resolutely rushed to the Qinghai-Tibetan plateau and calmly commanded flood control on site. In 1984, he led a team to Japan to attend the annual meeting of the International Commission on Large Dams (ICOLD). To save expenses, he lived in the Chinese embassy instead of a high-end hotel. He bought bread in the embassy for breakfast instead of having the meals from the conference. He ate noodles in diners for lunch and had dinners at the embassy canteen. At the time, the Three Gorges Project was about to launch, while many Japanese businessmen came to inquire about opportunities for collaboration. Li E'ding greeted everyone with courtesy but firmly refused any gifting.

LI EDING (1918–2001), born in Tianjin, was a member of the Communist Party of China. He was an expert in hydropower engineering, an academician of the Chinese Academy of Engineering, and a former Chief Engineer of the Ministry of Water Resources.

Li E'ding graduated from Tsinghua University in 1940 and studied in the UK. After the People's Republic of China was founded, he started working in the survey team of the State Administration for Hydropower Construction of the Ministry of Petroleum Industry. In the 1950s, he led technicians to survey, select sites, and plan accordingly in the upper and middle reaches of the Yellow River. He was one of the leaders who founded the hydropower survey team in China. In order to develop the cascade hydropower stations in the upper reaches of the Yellow River, Li E'ding once surveyed by walking along the Yellow River three times. He

Li E'ding

has not only promoted the hydropower development of the Yellow River but also advanced the research, planning, and site selection of national hydropower resources. In the past few decades, he has surveyed, selected the sites, and planned for many major rivers with rich hydropower resources in China, such as the Yellow River, the Yangtze River, the Hongshui River, the Lancang River, the Min River, the Xin'an River, the Ou River, the Yongding River and the Kashi River in Ili. He completed large amounts of preparatory work to develop hydropower resources in these rivers. He also participated in the site selection of Ertan Hydropower Station and Xiaowan Hydropower Station and the final selection of Sandouping as the dam site for the Three Gorges Project.

Li E'ding had worked in the hydropower construction industry for more than 50 years and was one of the pioneers of hydropower in New China. He once served as the Chief Engineer of Sanmenxia Hydropower Junction, the first large-scale hydropower station in the mainstem of the Yellow River. He was also the chief engineer of the 147-meter high Liujiaxia hydropower project, the first million-kilowatt hydropower station in China then. He also presided over the construction of hydropower stations, including Shizitan, Yanguoxia, Yingxiuwan, Maotiaohe, etc.

Li E'ding creatively solved many technical difficulties in the design, construction, and renovation of major projects and tackled the key technical problems in the rapid construction with mass concrete and complex foundation treatment of hydropower projects. For example, Shizitan Hydropower Project was the first project with mechanized construction in China then, which became a model for the control of future hydropower projects. The scheme reviewed by him solved the technical problems that had been widely determined as difficult in the international dam community, such as the design of foundation treatment for the complex weak fault zone of the left dam of the 178-meter high Longyangxia Arch Dam and the leak-proof foundation design of the 165-meter high Wujiangdu Dam with well-developed karst.

Liujiaxia Hydropower Station

Li Eding had been actively supporting and promoting advanced technologies from abroad and independent innovation achievements from China. For example, in the early 1970s, he actively guided, reviewed, and approved the in-dam powerhouse scheme of Fengtan Hollow Gravity Arch Dam, which led to the completion of the world's highest hollow arch dam; he proposed the new technology to adopt boring machine for the first time and led the manufacturing the first tunnel boring machine in China. In the early 1980s, he first proposed to promote the use of roller compacted concrete dam and faced rockfill dam, which had been particularly effective in saving cost and shortening construction schedule. After years of efforts, China's construction capability of these two types of dams in China has ranked among the top in the world.

Li Eding strongly supported reforming the hydropower construction system. He paid special attention to construction quality management and trained talents to participate in international competitions. He guided the construction of China's first World Bank loan-financed project (Lubuge Hydropower Project) to completion. In terms of construction management, the project adopted the bidding contracting system and supervisory engineer system for the first time.

Li E'ding strongly advanced the establishment of the National Large Dam Safety Supervision Center and formulated dam safety regulations. His suggestions for accelerating the development of medium-sized hydropower projects were adopted by the government. He attended the annual meetings of ICOLD many times and was elected as the vice chairman of ICOLD and the honorary chairman of the Chinese National Committee on Large Dams. As one of the pioneers of new China's hydropower undertakings, Li E'ding has made great contributions with his abundant knowledge, enthusiasm for hydropower, and innovative spirit.

WANG WENSHAO

Who Studied for the Sake of China and Its People

"Our great motherland has a long-standing brilliant culture as well as a quite long miserable experience. I went to study in the States bearing the idea of 'Save China with Science' in mind and obtained a doctoral degree. I always have the belief that I cannot forget the cultivation of my motherland and its people. It is unacceptable not to repay their kindness of supporting my studies by working diligently. I cannot forget that I'm a descendant of the Yellow Emperor, and I'm determined to dedicate to the people of my motherland after my graduation," In his article "The Kindness of Warm Sun Cannot be Repaid by Grass," Wang Wenshao wrote, "Studying abroad is inseparable from loving the motherland. We should not only learn from the world but also serve our motherland." In the latter years of his life, he said, "Although I have worked hard over the years, I always feel that I have done too little for the people to repay the kindness of my motherland."

WANG WENSHAO (1919–2007), born in Suzhou, Jiangsu Province, is a member of the Communist Party of China. He was an expert in earth mechanics, earth dams, and foundation seismology. He was also an academician of the Chinese Academy of Sciences, a professor of Engineering, and a doctoral supervisor of the China Institute of Water Resources and Hydropower Research.

Wang Wenshao

In 1943, Wang Wenshao graduated from the School of Hydraulic Engineering of the National Central University in Chongqing and volunteered to go to Gansu, Ningxia, and other northwest regions with difficult conditions to engage in irrigation and water conservancy work. In 1946, he served as a teaching assistant at National Central University in Nanjing and then went to study in the United States. While studying in the States, Wang Wenshao worked hard and earned a master's degree in mechanics and hydraulics from the University of Iowa two years later. In 1952, he obtained a doctorate in civil engineering from the Illinois Institute of Technology. He later served as an Assistant Researcher, then a Researcher at the Massachusetts Institute of Technology (MIT).

In 1949, the People's Republic of China was founded, and Wang Wenshao actively prepared to return home. However, civil war broke out in North Korea, and the Chinese People's Volunteer Army entered the DPRK to participate in the war and defend national security, which made it difficult for the students in the United States to return. In November 1950, Wang Wenshao was pressed by the Immigration Office in Chicago to renew his visa. The agency revoked his entry permit and banned him from leaving the United States. He then spent some time working at MIT, during which he was investigated by the FBI. In 1955, thanks to the efforts of the Chinese government, Wang Wenshao, together with other students studying in the United States, finally returned to the motherland they had been missing all the time. After he returned, he first worked in the Nanjing Hydraulic Laboratory of the Ministry of Water Resources, then the Hydraulic Research Institute of the Ministry of Water Resources.

To meet the national demand for hydraulic and hydropower engineering construction and safety, Wang Wenshao mainly engaged in the research of hydraulic and hydropower engineering construction as well as the earthquake damage analysis of hydraulic structures. He has made groundbreaking achievements in the dynamic characteristics, testing technology, dynamic analysis theory, and safety evaluation method of soil under earthquake loading. In 1959, Wang Wenshao was responsible for founding the research group studying "Liquefaction Issues of Saturated Sand" and established the first laboratory specialized in soil dynamics in China. He presided over the development of the first domestic vibration triaxial apparatus. In 1962 and 1964, Wang Wenshao published "Dissipation and Diffusion Issues of the Vibration Pore Water Pressure of Saturated Sand" and "The Mechanism of the Generation, Development and Dissipation of Vibration Pore Water Pressure of Saturated Sand," respectively. He took the lead in expounding the mechanism of generation, development and dissipation of pore water pressure of saturated sand under cyclic loading at home and abroad, which attracted the attention of international peers.

Wang Wenshao paid great attention to connecting the theory to practice and particularly emphasized the importance of going to the earthquake scene for damage investigation. Taking the risk of aftershocks, he went deep into Xingtai, Haicheng, Linger, and Tangshan to investigate the earthquake damage on site and participated in the compilation of *The Damage Caused by Tangshan Earthquake*. He spent four years compiling the *Compilation of Earthquake Damage Data of Hydraulic Projects in China (1961–1985)*, which comprehensively reflected the earthquake damage phenomenon and lessons learned from hydraulic projects during strong earthquakes from 1961 to 1985 in China. During 1980 and 1983, he served as the first director of the Institute of Aseismic Protection of the Institute of Water Resources and Hydropower Research. He extensively summarized the seismic damage data and engineering experience. He put forward the important conclusion that "engineering measures are more reliable than theoretical calculation and the variance analysis is more meaningful than the stability analysis," which established the ideas and principles of seismic design of Chinese earth dams and foundations and has significance in guiding the seismic design of earth dams in China.

LIN BINGNAN

Who Switched from Arts to Science and Devoted His Whole Life to Hydraulics

At the age of 90, Lin Bingnan once said, "In recent years, especially with the leadership of the Party, the progress of China is undeniable after the reform and opening up. I am very happy to live in such an era. We didn't expect China's development to be this good when we returned from abroad... At the time, I thought about when China could catch up with the United States and the United Kingdom with such low steel production. Now China's annual steel production reaches 500 million tons, ranking the top in the world. Our country is changing very fast thanks to the leadership of the Communist Party."

LIN BINGNAN (1920–2014), whose family was from Putian, Fujian, was born in Malaysia and later returned to China with his parents to settle in Guangzhou. He was an expert in hydraulics and river dynamics and one of the important founders and pioneers of the hydraulics discipline in China. He was an academician of the Chinese Academy of Sciences, a member of the Communist Party of China, and a senior engineer and honorary president of the China Institute of Water Resources and Hydropower Research.

Lin Bingnan planned to study liberal arts, influenced by his father. However, witnessing the weakness and poverty due to Japan's aggression towards China, he deeply felt the importance of developing national industry and switched his major from arts to science. In 1942, Lin Bingnan graduated with honors from the Department of Civil Engineering of

Lin Bingnan

Tangshan Engineering College of Northern Jiaotong University. After serving as a teaching assistant for a year, he went to Xiuwen Hydropower Project Office in Guizhou Province to work as an engineer, starting his career in hydraulics.

Lin Bingnan studied in the United States in 1946, then received both a master's degree and a doctor's degree in hydraulics from the University of Iowa. He taught at Colorado State University for a while, during which he never forgot his intention to return to China to develop water conservancy. After twists and turns, with the efforts of the Chinese government and international students, he took his family aboard the ship upon receiving the release notice.

After returning to China, Lin Bingnan worked in the Hydraulic Research Office of the Chinese Academy of Sciences. In 1958, the newly-built Hydraulic Institute of the Institute of Hydraulics was established. He served as the deputy director and adjusted his research direction to the high dam hydraulics research as per work demand.

Lin Bingnan was the first scholar in China to carry out the experimental model test of sudden drainage of the water body. In order to ensure the safety of both banks of the high dam, he began to study the routing problems of the dam-break flood, which provided important theoretical support for studying and solving the issues of Three Gorges protection later on.

Lin Bingnan developed a contractible new energy dissipation theory, including the study of the wide-flange pier and slit-type flip buckets, which provided an effective method for high dam energy dissipation, particularly those constructed in deep canyons. It has been successfully applied to many large hydropower projects such as Panjiakou, Ankang, Longyangxia, and Dongjiang. He also proposed that under certain conditions, a non-smooth surface can be adopted for the section of partial overflow downstream of the wide-flange pier to simplify the construction. This achievement collectively won the second prize of the State Science and Technology Advancement Award.

Lin Bingnan personally led the construction of the first large-scale active high-speed water flow aerated chute in China. The novel conception and ingenious design shown in the design of its key components, such as the movable joint of its water supply pipeline and the accelerated expansion section of the guide vane, have made it one of the most advanced hydraulic equipment in the world. In the 1970s, when he was cooperating with the Zhejiang Surveying Institute of Estuary and Coast to conduct the tidal current calculation in Hangzhou Bay, he combined the two-dimensional characteristic theory with the characteristic eccentricity difference scheme, which led to calculation results with good accuracy and stability. In the early 1980s, he first applied the two-dimensional feature theory to calculating large bays and estuaries and then promoted it across China.

In terms of sediment research, Lin Bingnan was the first to prove the existence of the concentration effect with a highly accurate experiment while studying the impact of sediment concentration and particle Reynolds number on sediment settling velocity. He also carried out a large amount of sediment transport tests in the flume, which achieved breakthrough progress. He participated in the complete process of the demonstration and construction of the Three Gorges Project. He served as the leader of the sediment demonstration expert group. He proposed the scheme to have the reservoir control the sediment deposition to guarantee the project's long-term benefits. He also proposed a double flood water control level as the dispatching method of the Three Gorges reservoir to effectively increase storage capacity, improve flood control safety, and divert sea water to deepen the estuary section of the lower Yellow River. Under his leadership, sediment, the key technical problem of the Three Gorges Project, was finally solved.

Lin Bingnan devoted his whole life to the scientific research of hydraulics and river dynamics, especially in high dam hydraulics, unsteady open-channel flow, and sediment movement.

CHEN JIYU

The Founder of China's Estuarine Coastal Studies

When later recalling the significance of the geological and economic investigation along the Hunan-Guizhou-Yunnan and Sichuan-Guizhou railways which he participated in 1950, Chen Jiyu said, "The greatest significance of the trip is its contributions to the country. I have to achieve whatever the country needs. Graduating from the History and Geography major, I completed a road map and production report by functioning as a compass, a hammer, and a prism. But I was truly happy as I was walking through the Hmong area, going deep into the mountains and forests during the trip. Because the country has just been liberated, many children would sing, 'The sky in the liberated area is bright.' A new China with a positive atmosphere was what we felt during the trip."

CHEN JIYU (1921–2017), who was from Guanyun, Jiangsu Province, was a member of the Communist Party of China (CPC). He was the founder of estuarine and coastal studies in China. He was an academician at both the Chinese Academy of Engineering and the International Eurasian Academy of Sciences. He was also a professor and lifelong professor of the Estuarine and Coastal Research Institute of East China Normal University.

Chen Jiyu

Chen Jiyu spent his childhood on the riverbanks and seaside of Guanyun, where the river channels, ports, and ships became his important childhood memories. He had been interested in the geographical atlas from a young age, while his deep geographical complex has sprouted as well.

Chen Jiyu had a difficult academic experience. After leaving his hometown, he traveled all the way from Shashi to Chongqing. He completed high school under difficult conditions, like the bombing of Japanese planes. He was admitted into the School of History and Geography of Zhejiang University and obtained a postgraduate degree in 1947. He wrote *The Topography of Hangzhou Bay* in the same year, which marked the official beginning of his estuarine and coastal studies and became the first study of estuarine development in hydrodynamics and sedimentology.

After the founding of the People's Republic of China, he participated in various field investigations and research while undertaking teaching tasks at the School of Geography at Zhejiang University. After completing the investigation along the Hunan-Guizhou-Yunnan and Sichuan-Guizhou railways, he focused on developing the Huai River regulation project. Meishan Reservoir, located on Shi River, a tributary of Huai River, was the highest multi-arch dam in the world built domestically at that time. Chen Jiyu also contributed to the construction of this project with his wisdom and painstaking efforts.

In the wave of "March forward to Science," Chen Jiyu founded the earliest estuarine and coastal research institution in China and gradually established the estuarine and coastal discipline system combining dynamics, sedimentation, and landform. In the past few decades, he devoted himself to studying the development and evolution of estuaries, the formation of underwater delta and estuarine bar, the historical and modern evolution of the coast, the profiling of muddy coast, and other theories. He made significant achievements in estuarine regulation, coastal engineering, coastal port planning and construction, hydropower engineering environment, and developing and utilizing the coast and tidal flats. His published work, *The Development Model of Yangtze River since 2000* and *The Development of Yangtze River Estuary and Delta*, provided a scientific basis for the regulation of the Yangtze River estuary.

From the 1950s to the 1980s, Chen Jiyu was one of China's main advocates of the comprehensive survey of the coastal zone and marine resources. He was also responsible for the pilot survey of the Wenzhou coastal zone as well as the principal of developing the major survey technical specifications and survey results report. The investigation found out the characteristics of the natural environment, the social and economic conditions of China's coastal zone, and the quantity, quality, spatial distribution, and temporal change of marine resources. It provided a solid and reliable scientific basis for the reasonable development of coastal zones, marine resources, and the protection of the coastal zone environment.

Chen Jiyu was always dedicated to the estuary and coast research. Whatever he proposed, be it the proposal of "Store Water in Dike" for the Huai River regulation project, or the various ideas he developed for the site selection of Pudong Airport, the development of a bridge in North Pudong and a tunnel in South Chongming Island, was based on the national demand with strong practical characteristics. Therefore, he was honored by Academician Shi Yafeng as "A great scientist who sticks to China's construction." He was awarded the first "Chinese Geography Achievement Award" by the Chinese Geographical Society in 2004 and the "Lifetime Achievement Award" by the International Estuarine and Coastal Society in 2013.

TAN JINGYI

An Academician in Hydraulics and a Master in Dam Construction

In 1982, Tan Jingyi, over 60 years old, honorably joined the Communist Party of China. On the day of joining the Party, Tan Jingyi was so excited that he wrote a poem at night, "My whole life is to regulate mountains and rivers, and I spent uncountable years in Fujian, Guangdong, Hunan, and Guizhou as it's my life goal to conquer nature; I have no regret aging as the new chapter of China's hydraulic development bring me so much happiness. While the stormy waves still linger in my dream, the high gorges and flat lakes are in view; I would stay fighting for the Four Modernizations wholeheartedly and persistently."

TAN JINGYI (1921–2016), born in Hengyang, Hunan Province, was a member of the Communist Party of China (CPC). He was a founder, pioneer, and leader of hydropower construction technology in New China as well as an expert in hydropower engineering and construction. He was an academician of the Chinese Academy of Engineering who was praised as "The Academician Comes from the River." In 2013, he was listed by the Publicity Department of CPC as one of the nine outstanding scientists of the Chinese Academy of Sciences and the Chinese Academy of Engineering.

As a student, Tan Jingyi worked extremely hard. During the War of Resistance Against Japan Aggression, he devoted himself to military service and gave up the superior benefits of the army after the victory of the war to realize his deal of saving the nation through science and

Tan Jingyi

technology. After graduating from Tangshan Engineering College of Northern Jiaotong University in 1946, Tan Jingyi devoted himself to hydropower project construction with enthusiasm. He participated in the construction of Gutianxi Hydropower Station, the first underground hydropower plant built after the founding of the People's Republic of China.

In 1956, Tan Jingyi moved to Lingnan as a chief engineer and participated in the construction of the Liuxihe Hydropower Station in Guangdong Province. This was the first double-curvature concrete arch dam domestically designed and constructed in China. For the first time, measures such as artificial coarse aggregate, concrete mixing and adding ice, and burying cooling water pipes inside the dam were adopted, which successfully solved the construction difficulties and achieved the goal of no cracks in the entire dam and no leakage in the dam foundation grouting gallery.

Since 1969, the team led by Tan Jingyi has made great efforts during the construction of Wujiangdu Hydropower Station, and achieved more than 600 scientific and technological achievements, including more than 20 major achievements. His team initiated the high-pressure grouting technology with Chinese characteristics, achieved outstanding results, and promoted the technology nationwide, which paved the

Wujiangdu Hydropower Station

way for the construction of high dams and large reservoirs in karst areas. In 1984, Wujiangdu Project won the silver prize in National Quality Engineering Award and won the first prize in the State Science and Technology Advancement Award in 1985.

Starting from 1982, at the age of sixty, he led technicians to conduct a series of technical research and built the highest thin double-curvature concrete arch dam at the time, the Dongjiang arch dam in Hunan Province, which was designed and constructed domestically. The project is of excellent quality and also marks the start of the mature period of Chinese arch dam construction technology.

As the first group of hydraulic engineering experts in New China, Tan Jingyi presided over the construction of eight dams, with a total installed capacity of 1.63 million kilowatts. He also participated and provided technical consultation for 80 dams. His sweat was shed on large and medium-sized hydropower stations such as the Three Gorges, Xiluodu, Wujiangdu, Dongjiang, Wuqiangxi, Shaoshan Irrigation Area, Ouyanghai Irrigation Area, and other hydraulic projects. His footprints were left on the Yangtze River, Yellow River, Jinsha River, Wu River, and all other kinds of rivers such as the Xiang River, Zi River, Yuan River, and Li River.

In China's hydropower construction, whenever technical and construction problems arise, Tan Jingyi was the first person that came to people's mind. He was called "Son of the River" and "Dam Master" with his footprints all over the rivers in China. Tan Jingyi is a participant and witness of the hydropower development in China. He was also a founder, pioneer, and leader of hydropower construction technologies in China. He has devoted his whole life to the undertakings of

The arch dam of Liuxihe Hydropower Station

hydropower development in China and the Party as well as the "Chinese Dream." He was a paragon of China's hydropower development undertakings and a model for hydropower developers.

QIAN NING

Who Aspired to Clear Water and Peaceful Rivers

During a lecture at Tsinghua University for students who were probationary party members and active applicants for CPC membership, Mr. Qian mentioned the night when the Chinese football team defeated the Kuwaiti football team and how the cheers erupted on the Tsinghua campus had him emotional. At that time, as a foreign student in the United States, he deeply hoped that the Chinese could be soon called "Healthy Man of East Asia" instead of "Sick man of East Asia!" And such hope was eventually realized under the leadership of the Communist Party of China. He couldn't help saying, "How lovely our China is! How lovely our youth are!" Everyone is responsible for revitalizing China!

QIAN NING (1922–1986) was born in Hangzhou, Zhejiang, and was a member of the Communist Party of China. He was an expert in sediment movement and riverbed evolution, an academician of the Chinese Academy of Sciences, and a professor at the Department of Water Resources of Tsinghua University.

Mr. Qian graduated from the National Central University in Chongqing in 1943. He studied in the United States in 1947 with a master's degree from the University of Iowa and a doctorate from the University of California. He learned from Hans Albert Einstein, the son of the famous physicist Einstein and an authoritative professor of sedimentology. They jointly published several academic papers, among which the movable bed sediment simulation test method they jointly proposed was called the Einstein-Chien Ning method. In 1951, Qian Ning began working as

Qian Ning

an assistant and associate research engineer at the Institute of Engineering Research of the University of California. However, this young scholar from the south of the Yangtze River in China was well aware of the serious problem of river sediment in his motherland, and the development of New China urgently needs talents to solve such problems. Thus, he had long established the goal to return to China and devote himself to developing his motherland.

Qian gave up his superior life in the United States, returned to the motherland in 1955, and worked in the Chinese Academy of Sciences Institute of Hydraulic Engineering. There, he participated in founding the Hydraulic Research Institute of the Chinese Academy of Sciences and served as the deputy director. In the late 1950s, the state began to build the Sanmenxia Reservoir and Liujiaxia Hydropower Station. The river regulation of the lower reaches of the Yellow River urgently needed to be carried out. Qian Ning then put all his efforts into regulating the Yellow River and its sediment.

Navigating in the torrential turbulence of the Yellow River, he asked the experienced river workers on the boat for advice. After observing and thinking, he conducted that the formation of the regular flow of the

Yellow River was due to the protruding mountain spur, dangerous section engineering, and naturally formed riverbend on the riverbank, which could contribute to embedded diversion. He named the natural or artificial flow control points on the banks of the Yellow River "nodes." Based on a large number of experiments, Qian Ning worked out a plan to regulate the lower reaches of the Yellow River through man-made "nodes." After a thorough investigation that accumulated rich information, he summarized the

Yellow River riverbed

evolution of the river channel and wrote *Riverbed Evolution of the Lower Reaches of Yellow River*, his first monograph after he returned to China. He presided over the study of the "Centralized Control of the Middle Reaches of the Yellow River Coarse Sediment Source Area," which is a breakthrough in understanding Yellow River regulation. He was thus known as the "Yellow River Expert."

Qian Ning carried out and advanced the research on the movement mechanism of hyper-concentrated flow, which made an important contribution to riverbed evolution research by combining river dynamics and geomorphology in China. In 1984, following his initiative, the International Centre for Training in Sediment Research was founded. He also launched the English edition of the *International Journal of Sediment Research*. Qian Ning established the sediment research laboratory of Tsinghua University, carried out research on fundamental theories of sediment, cultivated a large number of new talents, and provided strong support for the decision-making of major water hydraulic projects and river regulation projects nationwide.

Qian Ning mastered theories at a high level. He successively wrote books with theoretical and practical value, such as *Sediment Movement Mechanics* (first prize in National Book Award for Outstanding Scientific and Technological Book Award) and *Riverbed Evolution Theory*. He was also the chief editor of *Hyper-concentrated Flow Movement* (first prize in the National Science and Technology Book Award), and *Riverbed Evolution of the Lower Reaches of Yellow River*, which became valuable academic heritage for later generations.

Qian Ning was a scientist with deep theoretical accomplishment and a pioneering spirit. He has made important contributions to China's study of riverbed evolution, combining river dynamics and geomorphology and the regulation of the Yellow River. He advanced China's sediment research to a leading position internationally and laid a solid foundation for the scientific development of China's sediment science.

ZHANG WEIZHEN

The Pioneer of Farmland Irrigation

Zhang Weizhen, dedicated to teaching, answered all questions from his students and never kept important academic materials to himself. He was upright and selfless, never giving out gifts or accepting any. He lived a frugal simple, had an extremely simple diet, dressed plain, and had ordinary home decorations. But he was very generous to colleagues and students who had difficulties. He always responded to their requests and even initiated help sometimes. He was rigorous with his studies, sticking to academic ethics' bottom line, and never drifting with the wave. He would rather offend his partners or stay away from academic evaluation activities than deviate from the facts in his works.

ZHANG WEIZHEN (1923–2012), was born in Fengrun, Hebei (now Tangshan, Hebei). He was a member of the Communist Party of China and a hydraulic scientist and educator. He was an expert in groundwater and farmland irrigation projects. He was a pioneer of modern farmland irrigation discipline in China, an academician of the Chinese Academy of Engineering, a professor and a doctoral supervisor at Wuhan University, and a professor at Tsinghua University concurrently.

Zhang Weizhen studied in the Department of Civil Engineering of Peking University in 1941. In 1951, Zhang Weizhen was sent in the first batch to study at the Water Problems Institute of the Russian Academy of Sciences while teaching at Peking University after graduation.

Zhang Weizhen

There, Zhang Weizhen obtained the Candidate of Sciences degree with excellent grades. After returning to China, he was assigned to the Wuhan Institute of Hydraulic and Electric Engineering (now Wuhan University) to engage in teaching and researching farmland irrigation. Under his leadership, China's first farmland irrigation laboratory was established. He was also one of the first postgraduate supervisors of the farmland irrigation major in China and founded the first doctoral program in farmland irrigation discipline in China. He also edited the first textbook for farmland irrigation majors after the founding of the People's Republic of China and cultivated a large number of excellent talents in the field.

Zhang Weizhen's research mainly covered a wide range of irrigation-related topics, especially in aspects such as groundwater, soil water, and solute transport, where he not only proposed groundbreaking theory and calculation method but also successfully applied them in the practice of farmland drainage, saline-alkali soil improvement, and farmland source pollution reduction, etc. He was one of the first scholars in China to apply groundwater dynamics theory to farmland irrigation projects.

Zhang Weizhen devoted a large portion of his energy to the water conservancy and agriculture undertakings in Huang-Huai-Hai Plain, including farmland drainage and saline-alkali soil improvement. In the 1950s, secondary salinization of irrigated land was one of the thorny problems of farmland irrigation. He traveled to experimental districts all over Shandong, Henan, Hebei, and other provinces to quickly grasp the latest water and salt dynamics test information and carry out the pumping test.

Zhang Weizhen also made important contributions to the research and practice of the evaluation of groundwater resources. After a lot of field research conducted with other experts, they pointed out that the deep water in some areas of North China was basically "standing water" with a limited water supply. The groundwater exploitation should be mainly from shallow water. His view played an important role in guiding the rational development and utilization of groundwater resources in North China and other similar areas and establishing a correct concept of groundwater resources. The theory of "northern plain should mostly exploit its shallow water" was proved in practice. In 1978, "The Evaluation, Development, and Utilization of Groundwater Resources in North China Plain" won the National Science Conference Award.

Huang-Huai-Hai Plain

Zhang Weizhen is one of the advocates in China for studying solute transport from the viewpoint of applied dynamics. He put forward the calculation model of the groundwater desalination process between ditches, which provided a basis for scientific water management of irrigation areas threatened by secondary salinization in North China.

Zhang Weizhen was a member of the International Commission on Irrigation and Drainage and the expert group on the topics of the Twelfth and Fifteenth International Congress on Irrigation and Drainage. He devoted his whole life to teaching and researching farmland irrigation and groundwater resources and made groundbreaking contributions.

HU HAITAO

A Master of Engineering Geology

Hu Haitao was a famous master of engineering geology. He insisted on paying equal attention to theory and practice, creating the academic system of geology in China. He was a highly respected teacher who taught through percept and examples and had students all over the world. He was a romantic poet who praised the beautiful rivers and mountains of the motherland and left many excellent works. He was a calligrapher who wrote in simple, free technique with a powerful font. Hu Haitao has made outstanding contributions to the development of China's geology by depicting the country's vast territory with full enthusiasm.

HU HAITAO (1923–1998), was born in Zigong, Sichuan Province. He was a member of the Communist Party of China, an expert in engineering geology and environmental geology, and one of the first few academicians of the Chinese Academy of Engineering. He was also a researcher and honorary director of the Institute of Environmental Geology of the Ministry of Geology and Mineral Resources.

Hu Haitao

Hu Haitao graduated from National Central University in January 1946 and stayed there as a teacher. He successively served as the team leader of the Liao River Engineering Geology Team of the State Administration of Mineral Exploration of China Geological Work Plan Steering Committee and the deputy section chief of the Engineering Geology Department of Hydrogeology Engineering Geology Bureau of the Ministry of Geology etc. He went to the site in person to investigate the environment, which provided authentic and reliable data for constructing the project.

Hu Haitao was one of the great masters in the geology society in China and won several awards, such as the National Science Conference Award. He was good at thinking, not afraid to practice, and has thus made a great contribution to the geological work of constructing China's key projects with his continuous thinking and practice.

In the 1950s, Hu Haitao was responsible for the engineering geological survey of the comparison and selection of the dam area and dam section of the Three Gorges Project. He wrote the *Engineering Geological Survey Report on the Key Points of the Preliminary Design Stage of the Three Gorges Project*, carried out a large-scale supplementary survey of the project, and recommended Sandouping as the dam site for the Three Gorges Project's design. He also participated in writing the *Geological Seismic Demonstration Report of Yangtze River's Three Gorges Project*, which provided a theoretical basis for the safe operation of the project.

In the early 1960s, he conceived and compiled the first *China Engineering Geological Map* and studied the structure, construction, and stability of loess landslides in the Guanzhong region of Shaanxi Province.

The result of the study, together with the 1966 Xingtai earthquake geological study, became a model of applying geomechanics theories to solve engineering geological problems.

In the mid-1960s, Hu Haitao participated in the research on the relationship between the structural system along the Qinghai-Tibet Highway and the geological conditions of regional hydrogeological engineering and put forward the "water network theory," which won the National Science Conference Award.

From the end of the 1970s to the end of the 1980s, based on the project site assessment of geomechanics theory, Hu Haitao proposed the principles, methods, and steps for finding relatively stable blocks (also called "safety islands") as project sites in active areas as part of the site selection of Guangdong Province's Daya Bay and Liaonan Nuclear Power Station and the study of the regional crustal stability of the Heishanxia area of the Yellow River. This achievement has become one of China's important academic thinking for the evaluation of regional crustal stability of major projects.

In the 1990s, though late in life, Hu Haitao was still working hard for the major development in China, guiding many studies on hydrogeology, engineering geology, and environmental geology. He was one of the pioneers in studying environmental geology and disaster geology in China.

As a teacher, Hu Haitao attached great importance to the cultivation of talents and has developed a large number of excellent master's and doctoral students, which has cultivated future talents for the research of hydrogeology, engineering geology, and environmental geology in China.

Hu Haitao loved geology and was rigorous with his studies. He dedicated his life to China's hydrogeology, engineering geology, and environmental geology undertakings. He deserved to be called a master of geology.

QIAN ZHENGYING

The Daughter of Rivers

The past scenes flashed in Qian Zhengying's mind and became her spiritual power to spur herself to do more good deeds for the people. She said, "In the spring of 1991 when the National People's Congress approved the demonstration report of the Three Gorges Project, the Great Hall of the People was filled with applause. The applause reminded me of a lot about the past, including my father, when he came back from the United States with good wishes and was troubled by the fact that he could not realize them. He would have never imagined that his dreams eventually came true under the leadership of the Communist Party of China."

QIAN ZHENGYING was born in 1923 in Shanghai. She was a member of the Communist Party of China, an expert in hydraulics engineering, and an academician of the Chinese Academy of Engineering. She was a former minister of the Ministry of Water Resources.

Qian Zhengying's father was an expert in hydraulics. He received a master's degree in civil engineering from Cornell University and returned to China in 1922 to work on its development. Unfortunately, due to the bureaucratic corruption of Kuomintang, projects were constantly delayed. He eventually failed to achieve his ideal and aspirations. He

Qian Zhengying

advised his daughter to engage in architecture instead of hydraulics. But Qian Zhengying had long been influenced by him and was determined to develop water conservancy, control flood disasters, and serve the people after she grew up.

The legendary experience of the first woman minister of new China—who grew up with an "engineer dream" began in 1941, when she joined the Communist Party. Qian Zhengying grew up in the revolution team, during which she was tested by blood and fire.

In 1942, the underground organization of the Communist Party of China in Shanghai was destroyed. Qian Zhengying and other student Party members urgently evacuated to Huaibei Liberated District. The following year, the Huai River flooded. As a top student who majored in civil engineering, Qian Zhengying was appointed as the technical director to plug the breach and restore the levee. During the Chinese Civil War, Qian Zhengying returned to the frontier of hydraulic development at the end of 1947 after being an engineer for road and bridge construction for a year on the battlefield of Shandong Province. It seemed to be her destiny to become the daughter of rivers. In 1984, She served as deputy director of the Yellow River Affairs Bureau of Shandong Province, leading the regulation of the Yellow River. The Yellow River was the first stop where Qian Zhengying's water conservancy life actually began.

After the People's Republic of China was founded, Qian Zhengying successively served as vice minister of water resources of the East China Military and Political Commission and vice minister of the engineering department of the Huai River Regulation Commission. In 1954, a severe flood occurred in the Huai River basin. Qian Zhengying organized rescue with local cadres and groups, made decisions, patrolled, and defended the Bengbu dike. Subsequently, the state began to regulate the Huai River. Qian Zhengying, with Wang Huzhen—the minister of the engineering department of the Huai River Regulation Committee, and a large number of experts, planned and built a number of reservoirs in the upper reaches of the mainstem of the Huai River to intercept floods and develop water conservancy.

Between 1952 and 1988, Qian Zhengying successively served as the president of East China Water Conservancy College (now Hohai University), deputy minister of the Ministry of Water Resources and Ministry of Hydropower, and was elected vice chairman of the Chinese People's Political Consultative Conference (CPPCC). As one of the main decision-makers in China's water conservancy development, Qian Zhengying presided over the research and formulation of a series of principles, policies, and administrative measures on the development, utilization, management, and protection of water resources in China. She led the compilation of the regulation and planning of the Yellow River, the Yangtze River, the Huai River, and the Hai River and the long-term development outline of national water conservancy development. She also oversaw the completion of drafting the *Water Law of the People's Republic of China* and the *Water and Soil Conservation Law of the People's Republic of China*. She was in charge of the approval and decision-making of many major hydraulic and hydropower construction projects. She solved many significant technical difficulties during the construction of projects such as the Huai River Regulation Project, Miyun Reservoir, Liujiaxia Hydropower Station, and Gezhouba Hydropower Project. In the 1980s, Qian Zhengying was responsible for the demonstration of the Three Gorges Dam Project. She organized over 400 experts in various fields across the country to carry out an in-depth demonstration that lasted for two years and eight months, laying the foundation for the project's approval at the National People's Congress and its smooth construction.

She was elected academician of the Chinese Academy of Engineering in 1997. She then led a group of academicians to successively undertake six strategic consulting research projects on "water resources," for which she traveled across the country and obtained great achievements.

ZHAO GUOFAN

Who Had Gratitude for the Source of Benefit

Frugal but generous, this was Zhao Guofan's style as a master. He was rigorous, kind, and very caring. As a teenager, when the Japanese aggressors invaded China, he traveled halfway through China and finally completed his studies. Because he knew the hardships of his study, he took special care of the students with family difficulties. He once donated the RMB 100,000 prize of Chen Jiageng's technical science award to his teacher—Academician Qian Lingxi, who initiated the "Qian Lingxi Mechanics Award Foundation" to support students with difficulties. Zhao Guofan was also grateful to those who helped him. He often says, "When drinking water, one must think of its source."

ZHAO GUOFAN (1924–2017) was born in Fenyang, Shanxi Province. He was a member of the Communist Party of China and an expert in civil and architectural structural engineering and concrete structures. He was also an academician of the Chinese Academy of Engineering and a professor and doctoral supervisor at the Dalian University of Technology.

Zhao Guofan

He graduated with a structural engineering major from the Department of Civil Engineering of Shanghai Jiaotong University in 1949. He started working in Qiqihar Railway Bureau in September of the same year and was soon transferred to the Department of Water Resources of Lanzhou University as a teaching assistant. In August 1950, Zhao Guofan was transferred to the Dalian Institute of Technology, starting his teaching and scientific research career in civil and architectural structure.

Zhao Guofan had been engaged in the research of structural reliability, the structure theory, and engineering application of reinforced concrete for a long time, which made important contributions to the formulation of engineering structural specifications for majors such as hydraulic engineering, port engineering, architecture, and bridge engineering as well as to the solution of key technical problems in the major engineering projects of the national "Seventh Five-Year" and "Eighth Five-Year" plans such as Sichuan Ertan Arch Dam, Guizhou Dongfeng Arch Dam, Puding Roller-compacted Concrete(RCC) Arch Dam, and Guangxi Longtan RCC Gravity Dam. He was particularly pioneering in the reliability analysis of engineering structures, fracture parameters of large-scale full-graded concrete specimens, and the research on the test and analysis of the strength of multi-axis force mass concrete and fiber concrete was of great significance.

Zhao Guofan and his team undertook the sub-topic "Research on the constitutive model of concrete under plane-strain state" under the special topic of "Seventh Five-Year Plan" and three sub-topics in the "Eighth Five-Year Plan," including "Characteristics and test methods of concrete strength and deformation under dynamic loading," "Research on macro-mechanical performance of full-graded concrete" and "Research on the composite and dynamic fracture characteristics of concrete." During the last ten years, under the Seventh and Eighth Five-Year plans, he studied the macro multiaxial static and dynamic behavior of arch dam concrete based on the characteristics of the Ertan arch dam, including its large volume, large aggregate (maximum particle diameter of 150 mm), and its location in seismic area as a full-graded (four-graded) arch dam which required the research to take its dynamic loading and multi-axis force into consideration. He also applied fracture mechanics to study the composite fracture characteristic of concrete types I and II as well as the dynamic fracture characteristics under the impact of the earthquake. These four sub-topics were recognized by the Ministry of Electricity as the level of "domestic leading level," "partially international advanced level," "advanced international level," and "partially international leading level," respectively.

The Puding RCC arch dam project, which Zhao Guofan's research group participated in during Eighth Five-Year Plan, was the highest dam in the world among all existing RCC arch dams before the interception in 1989. The project won the first prize in the State's Science and Technology Advancement Award. In addition, "Research on Static and Dynamic Fracture Characteristics of Concrete" won the State's Science and Technology Advancement Award in 1999. "Key Technology in High Arch Dam Construction—Research on Shape Optimization and Structural Design of High Arch Dam" won the first prize of the Science and Technology Advancement Award in the Ministry of Energy in 1991. "Key Technology of High Arch Dam Construction—Research on Properties of High-strength Mass Concrete Materials" won the third prize in the State Science and Technology Advancement Award in 1998. All projects were led by Zhao Guofan.

Zhao Guofan introduced the theory of limit state design in China as early as the 1950s and first proposed calculating the safety factor using the first-order second-moment method in the 1960s. In his monograph *Reliability of Engineering Structures*, he put forward the practical calculation method of reliability and the statistical model of loadings and resistance, which has great influence in academia with thousands of copies published. He completed a lot of pioneering and fundamental work for compiling a unified standard of reliability design of engineering structures in China. In the 1990s, Zhao Guofan's research group further proposed several research results, including the reliability analysis method in the generalized random fields considering the correlation of variables, the second-order second-moment method, the fourth-moment method, and the system reliability analysis method with higher accuracy as well as the fuzzy mathematical analysis of the reliability of the serviceability limit state. Zhao Guofan enjoyed a high reputation in engineering structure reliability and domestically reinforced concrete structure research. He was the founder of civil engineering structural reliability research and made great contributions to engineering structure research in China and the world.

ZUO DONGQI

Who Regulated Water and Educated People
through Enlightenment and Teaching

Zuo Dongqi studied in the Soviet Union, which broadened his vision and deepened his thoughts. In his spare time, he liked to write poems. His collection of poems and essays reflected his strong, consistent career dedication and sense of responsibility. Zuo Dongqi was kind, respectful, and willing to listen to others' opinions, which showcased his "team spirit," "civilian consciousness," and "pragmatic" style. Those qualities enabled Zuo Dongqi constantly embark on new journeys and bring people lasting inspiration.

ZUO DONGQI (1925–2014), born in Zhenjiang, Jiangsu Province, was a member of the Communist Party of China. He served as the deputy engineer of the State Administration of North China Hydraulic Engineering and the president of Hohai University.

Zuo Dongqi was born to a local scholarly family in Zhenjiang, where he was influenced by literature since childhood. The deep influence of his scholarly family helped develop his compassionate and just personality. After graduating from Shanghai Jiaotong University, Zuo Dongqi focused on the field of river regulation and worked in the State Administration of North China Hydraulic Engineering. While working in Tianjin, Zuo Dongqi joined the Communist Party of China in 1948, engaged in the underground work of the Party, and contributed to the coming liberation of North China.

Zuo Dongqi

After the founding of the People's Republic of China, Zuo Dongqi was sent to the Soviet Union as the first batch of overseas students. After he graduated and returned to China, Zuo Dongqi worked at East China Water Conservancy College (now Hohai University). Since then, Zuo Dongqi's life has been closely tied to undertakings in water.

Zuo Dongqi had been highly sensitive to the macroscopic water problem of China, with deep thinking developed throughout his career. He pointed out that quite a few water-related problems exist during the construction of many projects. China had to pay attention to these issues and explore them with further discussions. Zuo Dongqi's water regulation ideas were based on the broad national situation and had far-reaching influence.

In terms of Yellow River regulation, Zuo Dongqi proposed that "less water and more sand" was one of the major "natures" of the Yellow River. However, if the regulation emphasized the water volume increase to the extent that excess water could flush sand into the sea or the sand reduction was so high that siltation would disappear in the river channel, the regulation would advocate the formation of a "non-

Yellow River" first rather than perceive as the object to be regulated. On the contrary, to regulate the "historically formed earth suspended river situation" with modern technological level and the regulation experience China accumulated in the long term was not something beyond our reach, but with potential for great achievements.

Zuo Dongqi won many awards for his scientific research projects, including Daya Bay Nuclear Power Plant, China's first nuclear power plant to introduce overseas technology and fund construc-

Daya Bay Nuclear Power Station

tion. The model test of the port channel and water intake and drain outlet that Zuo Dongqi presided over won the first prize in the State Science and Technology Advancement Award. The technology of the geomechanics model test and its applied studies in dam construction, which was led by Zuo Dongqi and Xia Songyou, won the second prize of the State Science and Technology Advancement Award. Zuo Dongqi was also an outstanding educator. He had been long engaged in the scientific research and teaching of hydraulics and hydraulic structures. *The Hydraulic Design Manual*, the textbook *Hydraulic Structures*, and the monograph *Theory and Method of Model Test* that he edited are all classic works of their respective discipline in China. He worked his whole life in hydraulic and hydropower research and dedicated all his energy and painstaking efforts to China's water conservancy undertakings.

WEN FUBO

"The General of Water Regulation" on the Yangtze River

In ancient Chinese, "fubo" means the capability of taming large waves. Ma Yuan, who lived in the Eastern Han Dynasty, was awarded the title of "General Fubo." In 1972, Wen came to Beijing to meet Premier Zhou Enlai, during which he was encouraged by Premier Zhou and with high hopes pinned on him. He kept the Prime Minister's instructions in mind, dedicated himself to his beloved cause of the regulation and development of the Yangtze River, and made great achievements. Thus, he became an expert in water regulation who deserved to be called "General Fubo."

WEN FUBO (1925–2020), born in Taojiang County, Hunan Province, was a member of the Communist Party of China. He was an expert in hydraulic engineering, an academician of the Chinese Academy of Engineering, and a professor-level senior engineer of the Yangtze River Conservancy Commission of the Minister of Water Resources. He was also a former chairman of the Technical Committee of the Yangtze River Basin Planning Office.

Wen Fubo

In 1943, Wen Fubo graduated from high school with excellent grades and was admitted to the Department of Hydraulic Engineering of the National Central University in Chongqing. As every tree is valuable in the forest and each water drop counts in the river, hundreds of thousands of young people can make a huge army.

In 1944, he gave up writing and joined the military services. During the fall of 1946, Wen returned to the National Central University in Nanjing to resume his studies. In the strong modern academic atmosphere of the university, he not only gained professional knowledge but was also exposed to progressive ideas and actively participated in the activities held by progressive students. In 1948, he joined the Youth Society of New Democracy. In 1949, after the founding of the People's Republic of China, he joined the Communist Party of China.

In May 1949, Wen Fubo participated in the takeover of some colleges as the secretary of the College of the Culture and Education Committee of Nanjing Military Control Commission. But he always looked forward to the water conservancy undertakings. By September of the same year, he finally realized his wish and was assigned to work at the Yangtze River Conservancy Bureau. In May 1950, he was transferred to the State Administration of Yangtze River Hydraulic Engineering in Wuhan, thus starting his river regulation career for more than half a century.

During the construction of the Jing River Flood Diversion Project, Wen Fubo and his colleagues completed the design task of the two sluices and guided and supervised the construction quality. He also served as the secretary to the commander of the north sluice and the head of the construction quality inspection team. The task was urgent with a tight timeframe, but the construction quality must be guaranteed. Wen Fubo was meticulous and carried out the construction strictly with the drawings and design requirements. He contributed his strength to the completion of this large-scale project which was rarely seen in the world then, taking the first step after his career debut.

Danjiangkou Dam Project

After the flood diversion project of the Jing River, Wen Fubo participated in the construction of the Dujiatai flood diversion and storage project completed in 1956, the Danjiangkou Dam Project completed in 1958, and the Gezhouba Dam Project completed in 1970. In the past 50 years, Wen Fubo has made great efforts and contributed selflessly to regulating the Yangtze River and eradicating its flood risk, leading to a series of technological achievements. For example, the Danjiangkou Dam Project, the key project for the comprehensive regulation and development of the Han River, was not only the water source project of the Middle Route of South-North Water Diversion Project but also the first practice of transferring plain sluices construction to high dams and large reservoirs development in the history of Han River regulation. It was the largest and world-class hydropower station in China then. It was of great significance to the comprehensive planning of the Yangtze River basin and the development of the Three Gorges Project and all other high dams in China. Wen and his colleagues established themselves as a great model for the development history of the Han River. In constructing the following Gezhouba Project and Three Gorges Project, Wen Fubo also paid endless painstaking efforts and made great contributions. Wen Fubo was responsible for planning, demonstrating, designing, constructing quality inspection, and managing New China's major dam projects in the Yangtze River Basin. In 1994, he was elected as one of the first batches of academicians in the Department of Civil, Hydraulic, and Construction Engineering of the Chinese Academy of Engineering. He was also the first academician of the Yangtze River Conservancy Commission.

ZHOU JUNLIANG

Who Dedicated to Water Conservancy with Full Enthusiasm

Zhou Junliang contributed and worked for science and his favorite water conservancy undertakings at the cost of his life. For decades, he barely had a complete day off work; he had suffered from three GI bleeds and received two notices of critical illness. Even when the doctor gave up on him, he recovered tenaciously and said, "I cannot stop contributing to the Huai River!" At that time, he was investigating the Luoma Lake levee and the Sanhe Zha. A communist's value is often less reflected at the moment but more in constant dedication. Zhou Junliang, who took the oath to the Party flag during the white terror era, has always carried the spirit of the Communists in his design career for decades. He was strict in self-discipline and worked selflessly. He was fearless even when facing death.

ZHOU JUNLIANG, born in Wuxi, Jiangsu Province, in 1925, was a member of the Communist Party of China. He was an expert in the design of hydraulic and navigation engineering structures. He was also an academician of the Chinese Academy of Engineering, a senior engineer of the Water Resources Department of Jiangsu Province, and a consultant to its Expert Committee.

In 1949, Zhou Junliang graduated from the Department of Civil Engineering of Fudan University. After graduation, this 24-year-old young Communist Party member came to the North Jiangsu

Zhou Junliang

Administration of Agriculture and Water Office as an engineer and successively worked in the Cotton Reclamation Bureau of North Jiangsu Administration of Agriculture and Water Office and the Water Conservancy Bureau. From 1951 to 1955, he served as the head of the metal structure group of the North Jiangsu Huai River Regulation Headquarters. During this period, he dedicated the best of his youth to helping the people of northern Jiangsu with river regulation.

Zhou Junliang had been engaged in the design of hydraulic projects for a long time. Specifically, he was responsible for the planning and design review of more than 80 medium to large-sized hydraulic and shipping buildings in Jiangsu Province. He obtained many breakthrough achievements in hydraulic projects.

Zhou Junliang presided over the design of a major project, Zaohe No. 1 Pump Station. He successfully solved the project's technical problems, making the operation of the pumping station safe and reliable with a device efficiency higher than that of the most advanced pumping station at that time. The project also won the gold award of the State's Design Excellence Award. He presided over the design of Jiangdu's No. 3 and No. 4 Pump Station, which adopted a half-levee back style structure for the first time in China. It was a pump station with the highest efficiency and the lowest cost by unit flow at the time.

In addition, he presided over the design of the Wudingmen Pump Station, which adopted the two-way flow channel for the first time. It integrated pumping and irrigation, pumping and drainage, self-diversion, and self-drainage and won the silver award of the National Quality Engineering Project (team award). The reconstruction design of Jiangzhuang Submergible Sluice was the first to adopt the hydraulic automatic gate opening and closing in China. It achieved automatic flood discharge and water storage and was promoted across the country as a sluice. The design of Xinshu sluice was the first to adopt the inverted arch bottom plate

Gaoliangjian Sluice

and straight arch bridge structure in a sluice, which saved a great amount of steel and cement. The reinforcement design of Gaoliangjian Sluice and Sanhe Zha adopted the newly proposed approach of increasing the friction resistance between the bottom plate and the foundation, which turned out to be successful. The approach had been recorded in the *Design Specification for Sluice*. In the Wuxi Dushan Dam Project, Zhou Junliang initiated the navigation applicable arc-shaped lifting arch gate with sinking electric shaft synchronous opening and closing at variable speed, which won the silver award of the State Design Excellence Award.

During the construction of the Grand Canal, Zhou Junliang presided over and participated in designing seven large navigation locks of the first line of the canal's North Jiangsu Section Phase I. The design scale of all the locks was 2×3000 t fleet. The design level was leading in China by adopting variable speed water delivery at the head of the lock, various energy dissipation forms and centralized electrical control, and shortened time of ship passing through the lock. He was in charge of the design review of the navigation lock project of Phase II Project, participated in the construction guidance and completion acceptance, solved many technical problems, and successfully handled a variety of complex foundations. Among the navigation locks he participated in building, eight won the Jiangsu Province Design Excellence Award, and one won the State's Design Excellence Award. In 1972, Zhou Junliang participated in the design demonstration of Gezhouba's navigation lock. In 1978, he was awarded for outstanding scientific and technological contributions at the Jiangsu Science and Technology Conference. In 1989, the Ministry of Construction awarded him the "Chinese Engineering Design Master." He was a pioneer in the design of large inland river locks in China. His design methods of navigation locks and other hydraulic projects were written into the "Design Specification of Water Locks" and "Design Specification of Navigation Locks," which have made an important contribution to the development of waterway construction in Jiangsu Province, the development of rive channels and port engineering discipline in China, and the formulation of national technical standards for the structural design of hydraulic construction projects.

XIE JIANHENG

The Pioneer of River Sediment Engineering

On the eve of the founding of the People's Republic of China, Xie Jianheng was studying at Wuhan University. At that time, he was determined to contribute to regulating the sediment in the Yellow River and Yangtze River. In 1951, he went to the Soviet Union to study and officially set river sediment control as his research focus. He deeply felt that the soil erosion in the Yellow River basin is serious. The erosion, transport, and sediment deposition had brought immeasurable harm to people's lives and property. The sense of responsibility and deep love for the motherland and its people as a scientist made him pursue the cause of river sediment control.

XIE JIANHENG (1925–2011), born in Honghu, Hubei Province, was a member of the Communist Party of China. He was an expert on sediment and river regulation and an academician of the Chinese Academy of Engineering. He once served as the vice president of Wuhan Institute of Hydraulic and Electric Engineering (now Wuhan University), as well as a professor and doctoral supervisor of Wuhan University.

In 1946, Xie Jianheng was admitted to Wuhan University. Under the guidance of Professor Zhang Ruijin, he established the goal of conquering the Yellow River. After returning from aiding Vietnam's Anti-American War, he devoted himself to the theoretical research of river sediment movement mechanics, river evolution, and river simulation and his teaching work.

Xie Jianheng

From 1956 to 1965, Xie Jianheng mainly studied the Yellow River, summarized the influence of sediment on the wandering change of the river channels, and straightened out the lifting law of the suspended river. He repeatedly investigated along the Yellow River at the risk of his life and diagnosed Yellow River's "pulse." After his calculation, he summarized the experience, combined it with the field investigation, and proposed to adopt comprehensive means to regulate the Yellow River. He delved into the sediment problem of the Yellow River. He made a systematic and in-depth discussion on the estuary delta evolution of the Yellow River's lower reaches, the change of its longitudinal section, and the physical mechanism and regulation approaches of riverbed uplift. In 1970, Xie Jianheng switched his main research focus to the Yangtze River. In 1971, Xie Jianheng and his colleagues began to study the technology of sediment flushing in the approach channel of Gezhouba lock. He visited the construction site of the Gezhouba dam in Yichang many times, during which he determined the best direction of the scouring sluice based on the landform of Gezhouba, formulated the best scheme for the construction of the scouring sluice, and verified that Professor Zhang Ruijin's idea of "still water for ship navigation, dynamic water for sand flushing" was correct. In the fall of 1981, the scouring sluice of the Sanjiang Channel of Gezhouba was opened for the first time. In only 12 hours, more than three million cubic meters of sediment deposited on the approach channel were removed. The actual results tallied with the test results from Xie Jianheng. This achievement laid a foundation for future study of the Three Gorges Project sediment problems.

In 1982, Xie Jianheng was entrusted by the State's Science and Technology Commission and the Ministry of Hydropower to serve as the deputy head of the sediment expert group of the Three Gorges Project. He organized and coordinated the technical research on the sediment problem of the Three Gorges Project and

Gezhouba Scouring Sluice

presided over the model test of the water quality and bed load, which provided an important scientific basis for the macro-level policymaking of the Three Gorges Project. He completed many detailed investigations, experiments, and analyses with his colleagues, submitted numerous feasibility reports, and put forward the impact of scouring and silting on the channel and its solutions. He also gave out new advice on the water storage level scheme of the Three Gorges Project, which was taken seriously by the state.

He was one of the founders of the river sediment and river regulation engineering major at Wuhan Institute of Hydraulic and Electric Engineering (now Wuhan University) and trained many talents. *River Sediment Engineering*, which was edited by him, was the only complete set of sediment engineering textbooks in China at that time. Xie Jianheng has made outstanding contributions to the reform and development of the major.

XU QIANQING

Who Prevented the Flood and Disasters and Understood the World with a Clear Perspective

This was how Xu Qianqing summarized his life in his diary, "I'm just a mediocre hydraulic professional, not an expert at all. I worked diligently for my whole life but only made a few achievements. But I spared no efforts to do what I could and live up to the food offered by peasants and the clothes and daily supplies given by workers. I didn't do anything that hurt my friends and family in my entire life, so I can probably be called an average laborer who lived his life with a clear conscience."

XU QIANQING (1925–2010), born in Chenggu, Shanxi Province, was a member of the Communist Party of China (CPC). He was an expert in flood control engineering and water conservancy planning, an academician of the Chinese Academy of Engineering, and a former deputy chief engineer of the Ministry of Water Resources.

In early September 1949, Xu Qianqing, who was 23 at the time, graduated from the Department of Civil Engineering of Shanghai Jiaotong University and was assigned to the Water Conservancy Office of the North Jiangsu Administration in Taizhou, where his water conservancy

Xu Qianqing

career started. From 1949 to 1953, he served as a technician in the Water Conservancy Office of the North Jiangsu Administration in Taizhou and the Ministry of Water Resources of East China and was transferred to the Ministry of Water Resources in April 1953. From 1953 to 1958, he served as a technician in the Soviet Union Expert Studio and Science and Technology Committee of the General Office of the Ministry of Water Resources. He successively served as the engineer and deputy director of the State Administration of Water Resources and Hydropower and the Planning Bureau of the Ministry of Water Resources. He also worked as the director of the Science and Technology Department, the deputy director of the Science and Technology Commission, the deputy director of the Science and Technology Department of the Ministry of Water Resources, and the deputy director of the Planning Department of the Ministry of Water Resources. In 1988, he became the deputy chief engineer of the Ministry of Water Resources.

Xu Qianqing had been engaged in the work of fields including water conservancy planning, river regulation, flood control and disaster reduction, water resources and environment, construction of major projects, and water science and technology development.

In terms of flood control and disaster reduction, Xu Qianqing presided over and participated in the compilation and review of all previous flood control plans for the seven major rivers in China and suggested planning from a strategically advantageous position, a planning idea that became a strategic guidance for the comprehensive flood control planning of the basin. He pointed out that flood control and river regulation should be closely linked to each other, "China's flood control is the regulation of its seven rivers in certain aspects." He advanced and joined all previous comprehensive planning of large rivers and successively served as the leader of expert groups of national scientific research projects of the Eighth Five-Year Plan and the Ninth Five-Year Plan, including Regulation of the Yellow River, Flood Control of the Yangtze River, Development and Utilization of Water Resources in Northwest China. He also presided over the research of the Ministry of Water Resources, Water and Sediment Change project in the Yellow River Project, of which the results were applied in the planning of the regulation of the Yellow River and the flood control of the Yangtze River.

Xu Qianqing was the editor-in-chief of the *Water Conservancy Encyclopedia China* and *Water Resources Volume · China Water Encyclopedia*. He edited and reviewed fundamental monographs such as *Chinese Terms in Water Conservancy* and wrote dozens of articles such as "China's Flood Control," "China's Water Conservancy in the 21st Century—Comprehensive Development with a City-centered Approach," and "Review and Discussion of Several Water Conservancy Issues in China."

Xu Qianqing conducted deep research on water resources issues in Northwest China and proposed ten relations that the large-scale development of western development had with water, which had great significance in guiding Western China and the capacity development of water resources in Western China. Xu Qianqing also carried out research on the water shortage in North China and gave several suggestions to alleviate water shortage and guarantee water security in Beijing.

Xu Qianqing also made great contributions to the demonstration, planning, design, and construction of the South-North Water Diversion Project and the Three Gorges Project. "The South-North Water Diversion Project is a strategic measure to alleviate the shortage of water resources in the Huang-Huai-Hai Basin. But the scope of water supply and the scale of water diversion should be clarified," he said. He proposed to handle the relationship between water transfer and the ecological environment well. In the Three Gorges Project, he was appointed as a member of the leading demonstration group and concurrently the leader of the flood control expert group. He was responsible for demonstrating the Three Gorges Project's effect on the flood control system of the Yangtze River and the overall arrangement of the flood control planning of the middle and lower reaches of the Yangtze River.

LIU JIZHOU
Who Saved the World with Water Conservancy and Stayed through Difficulties with the People

When Liu Jizhou just joined the construction of the Xiamen seawall project, the city's coastal areas were often interfered with by Kuomintang's aircraft bombing. Although the anti-aircraft artillery units offered protection, its air military force was still weak compared to the enemy's. More than 150 dyke construction workers and cadres had been killed. Under such extremely difficult conditions, Liu Jizhou and other construction workers stick to their positions with continuous construction at the risk of their lives. When he was building the Port of Rizhao, a local resident asked him when he would have a TV set at home. He replied, "Soon. Once the port was built, we would have everything." He always remembered this conversation where he deeply felt the great significance of the Communist Party of China leading the Chinese people to build socialism.

LIU JIZHOU (1926–2011) was from Luan County, Hebei Province (now Luanzhou City, Hebei Province). He was a member of the Communist Party of China, an expert in civil and water transportation engineering, and an academician of the Chinese Academy of Engineering. He successively served as the deputy director, the director, and the chief engineer of the Infrastructure Bureau of the Ministry of Transportation and Communications.

Liu Jizhou graduated from Tientsin Kung Shang College, where he received advanced training in civil discipline, participated in the student movement, and set the

Liu Jizhou

grand goal of developing the country after his completion. After the founding of the People's Republic of China, Liu Jizhou's career in navigation finally began with the construction of Tianjin's Port of Tanggu. He was assigned to work area I for building the breakwater. He actively studied and exercised to accumulate experience and improve his professional level, striving to grow into a "real proletarian engineer" soon. After 1950, he quickly grew up during the construction of the Port of Nanjing and Port of Tanggu and joined the Communist Party of China in 1952. In 1953, he participated in the construction of the Xiamen Seawall Project, completed the calculation and analysis of wave data, the design of the body section and top layout of the embankment, and was in charge of the prefabrication and installation of the first caisson in New China. The project adopted the new underwater explosion ramming technology for the first time in its construction, which was then incorporated into the industry standards of the People's Republic of China. During the construction, Liu Yizhou and his colleagues repaired the dike under the artillery fire of the Kuomintang aircraft. He also fully took the leading role as an excellent young Party member by enthusiastically helping the young interns and workers.

During the first craze of port construction in China, Liu Jizhou organized and presided over the site selection, planning demonstration, feasibility study, preliminary design, and approval of each coastal port. He reviewed and participated in the construction of important projects. For example, he presided over the construction of the Port of Rizhao Phase I Project, which adopted the open (without breakwater) scheme and the new technology of launching the floating dock of the 3300 t caisson base. He also presided over the

Xiamen Seawall

installation and commissioning of the 70,000 t silo equipment of the Lianyungang bulk grain wharf. The achievements of the studies of him and his team, such as the reinforcement of vacuum preloading soft foundation, prestressed reinforced concrete large pipe pile, and construction with explosion method, reached advanced level in China and had been widely applied, which led to great economic and social benefits.

Liu Jizhou participated in the plan formulation and construction of the Port of Tianjin, Port of Qingdao, Port of Rizhao, Huanghua Port, and many other ports. He developed high-quality projects one after another with his painstaking efforts, especially the Huanghua Port Liquid Chemical Wharf, Huanghua Port Outer Channel Regulation, and the Nanwei Dike at Nanjiang Port Area of Port of Tianjin that he helped build.

The Qinhuangdao Coal Terminal Phase III Project and Shandong Port of Rizhao Coal Terminal Project, which Liu Jizhou participated in developing, both won the highest award in the construction industry, the Luban Prize. The terminal and container yard project on the north side of the Port of Tianjin's East Embankment won the second Tien-yow Jeme Civil Engineering Prize; The Port of Qingdao Qianwan Phase III Berth Project won both the Tien-yow Jeme Prize and Luban Prize.

In regard to academic achievements, organization, and summary, Liu Jizhou edited *Forty Years Development of Navigation Engineering Technologies*, which comprehensively introduced the history of the development of China's navigation engineering and the application of new techniques, new technology, new structure, and new materials. The book played a great role in advancing the development of China's navigation engineering construction.

CHEN ZHIKAI

A Hydraulic Professional Who Endured Hard Times

Chen Zhikai lived a simple life and cared about the growth of young people. He had always requested his name to be deleted or to be placed after the collaborator for many of the important scientific research projects he presided over, even when the projects were applying for science and technology awards from the Ministry of Water Resources and the state. His magnanimity and sincerity reflected the noble sentiment of a scientist. "Scientific researchers need to put themselves in the state's shoes," he said.

CHEN ZHIKAI (1926–2013), born in Shanghai, was a member of the Communist Party of China (CPC). He was an expert in hydrology, water resources, and hydraulic planning. He was also an academician of the Chinese Academy of Engineering (CAE) and once the director of the Water Resources Institute of the China Institute of Water Resources and Hydropower Research.

Chen Zhikai

Chen Zhikai graduated from Shanghai Jiaotong University in 1950 with a bachelor's degree in engineering. When the People's Republic of China was just founded, large-scale hydraulic construction was carried out in China, but the hydrological data were lacking, while the design flood, calculation methods, and standards were inconsistent. However, hydraulic structures' holding capacity of the flood is closely related to whether rare floods could be established as the design standard. Therefore, studying the calculation method of storm flood design became an urgent task. Chen Zhikai's research focuses thus shifted from hydraulic projects to storm floods. He put himself in the state's shoes and developed the fundamental research field of engineering hydrology, such as the storm flood in China.

Chen Zhikai has completed groundbreaking research in aspects including small watershed storm flood, water resources evaluation, four-water precipitation, water resources planning, etc. The results of the "Preliminary Evaluation of China's Water Resources" research project, led by Chen Zhikai, have filled the blank of domestic water resources evaluation theory and practice. Before the reform and opening-up, he was mainly engaged in the research on engineering hydrology, rainstorm, and flood. After the reform and opening-up, he started committing to the research and application of water resources evaluation and water resources planning.

In terms of hydrological research, Chen Zhikai mainly completed the research on "The Calculation Method of the Frequency of Chinese Storm Flood" and "The Calculation Method of Design Flood and Design Storm," which provided a scientific basis for the formulation of the *Code for Design Flood Calculation*.

He presided over and completed the compilation of the *Atlas of Rainstorm Parameters in China* and the *Atlas of Chinese Hydrology*, which won the National Award for Natural Science at the National Science and Technology Conference in 1978. In 1963 and 1975, he participated in the field investigation, report compilation, and national survey of a rainstorm in the upper reaches of Hai River and Huai River two times. From 1975 to 1978, he participated in the compilation of the *Calculation Method of the Possible Maximum Rainstorm in China* and the *Contour Plot of the Possible Maximum Rainstorm in China*, as well as the revision of the *Standard of Design Flood* and the *Code for Design Flood Calculation*. After 1979, he mainly studied the regional water resources in China. In 1981, to supplement the national agricultural regionalization work plan, he presided over the completion of the preliminary evaluation of China's water resources, which gained experimental experience for the approaches and methods of China's water resources evaluation as well as opened up China's water resources evaluation work and filled in its blank. The research result was awarded the second prize of the State's Science and Technology Advancement Award in 1985. Since 1980, the Beijing-Tianjin-Hebei-Shandong and other regions had been subject to continuous drought and water resources crises. As the principal person in charge, he completed the research on the quantity, quality, and available amount of the water resources in North China. He also put forward the "four-water precipitation" (precipitation-surface water-soil water-groundwater) transformation relationship model through numerous experiments and research, which provided a scientific basis for unifying the evaluation results of surface water and groundwater of various departments. The subject won the third prize in the State's Science and Technology Advancement Award in 1991.

From 1985 to 1990, Chen Zhikai presided over the completion of the "The Development and Utilization and Supply-Demand Balance Analysis of Water Resources in North China and Jiaodong Peninsula" project, which won the first prize of the Science and Technology Award of the Ministry of Water Resources. As a consultant of the Yellow River and Northwest China Water Resources Research Projects under the Eighth Five-Year Plan and the Ninth Five-Year Plan, he advocated associating water resources with regional macro-economy and the ecological environment when researching. During this period, he participated in the demonstration of the Three Gorges Project, the South-North Water Diversion Project, and a series of major international cooperation projects on water resources. He also participated in the "Research on the Water Resources Strategy for China's Sustainable Development," "Research on the Strategy of Water Resources Allocation, Ecological Built Environment and Sustainable Development in Northwest China," sponsored by the Chinese Academy of Engineering, and some other relevant special studies. Chen Zhikai made important contributions to China's design of engineering hydrology, the evaluation and planning of water resources, and the formulation and implementation of macro-strategies of water resources.

CAO CHUSHENG

The Pioneer of Dam Construction Design

Cao Chusheng believed that water conservancy and hydropower are great causes affecting national economic development and people's livelihood and safety. He said, "The success of every project requires honest and practical work of the people, careful consideration… and the quality of persistence." He always planned all his work considering the broad situation of the Party and the state. He served for scientific research work, focused on the major needs of the state, and actively undertook major national engineering and key technical research projects.

CAO CHUSHENG (1926–2017), born in Wuxi, Jiangsu Province, was a member of the Communist Party of China. He was an expert in water hydraulics and hydropower engineering design and hydraulic structures. He was an academician of the Chinese Academy of Engineering and has successively held the positions of deputy chief engineer and chief engineer at Beijing Investigation and Design Institute of the Ministry of Water Resources, Northwest Investigation and Design Institute, Sinohydro Corporation Engineering Bureau 5 and 13. He was also a professor at Tianjin University.

In 1944, Cao Chusheng was admitted to Shanghai Jiaotong University with the second-best score and started studying in the civil engineering department. After graduation, he stayed at the school as a teaching

Cao Chusheng

assistant for courses, including the high-grade reinforced concrete structure and elastic mechanics. He also engaged in designing some plants and bridges.

After the founding of the People's Republic of China, in response to the call to "go to where your motherland needs the most" and "Huai River must be regulated," Cao Chusheng led the senior students to regulate the Huai River, thus starting his career in water conservancy.

The projects designed by Cao Chusheng include Foziling multi-arch dam, Mozitan massive-head dam, Xianghongdian gravity dam, Yanguoxia hydropower station, Bikou dam, etc. Specifically, during the construction of the Yanguoxia hydropower station, the calculation method of the sliding of the dam body together with part of the soft foundation along the weak interlayer was put forward for the first time, which was considered innovative at that time. Cao Chusheng was a proponent of pumped storage technology who advanced the construction of hybrid pumped storage power stations, zero-slump roller compacted concrete dams, and micro-slump dams. He studied computer-aided design, virtual simulation calculation, and risk analysis of hydraulic and hydropower projects and made great progress in developing risk design and optimization design improvement. He participated in the review, consultation, and evaluation of major hydropower projects such as Three Gorges, Sanmenxia, Gongzui, Ertan, Xiaowan,

Lijiaxia, and Zipingpu. Most of the projects he participated in were major domestic projects and the first in their category. These projects had all endured earthquakes and floods, and most are still in good operation.

Cao Chusheng had long been engaged in detailed design work at the frontier. In the 1950s, under the guidance of Wang Huzhen, a famous hydraulic expert, Cao Chusheng was responsible for designing the Foziling multi-arch dam, Mozitan massive-head double buttress dam, and Xianghongdian gravity arch dam. The three dam types had distinctive characteristics, respectively, and were all the first domestic projects in their category. In the 1960s, Cao Chusheng presided over the design of the Yanguoxia hydropower station, the first water conservancy project on the Yellow River that balanced irrigation function and economic benefits. In the 1970s, he was responsible for the design of the Bikou dam, the first large-scale roller-compacted rockfill dam in China. In the 1980s, he designed the Panjiakou Dam Project, the overflow dam with a wide-flange tail pier was first adopted in China. It was also the first large-scale hybrid-storage power station in China.

Panjiakou Dam Project

Cao Chusheng's creative achievements in the hydraulic structures field made outstanding contributions to the construction of hydraulic projects in China. He actively devoted himself to the cause of Huai River regulation, served the construction of Northwest China's water conservancy, and committed himself to the development of modern dam engineering in China. He was bold and innovative in design conception, strict and meticulous with specific structural design and construction quality, and obtained remarkable achievements in creating and developing specific designs and structural types of various dams in China. He designed Panjiakou Dam and Shimantan Dam, which won the National Design Excellence Gold Award. In 1989, he won the title "Chinese Engineering Design Master."

LUO XIBEI

Who Devoted to the Rivers with Love for His Motherland

Before he fully recovered, Luo Xibei took a team to the Heishanxia reach of the upper reaches of the Yellow River for survey and design. He then went to the Longyangxia reach to build the Longyangxia hydropower station. The area was uninhabited for generations, 3600 meters above sea level, with a deficit of one-third of its oxygen level. It was also the infected area of the No. 1 disease (plague). The hypoxia caused by high altitude had Luo Xibei, who had been working all day, too weak even to close the door. But he never complained. Perhaps, deep in his heart, his father, who sacrificed for the country, was quietly encouraging him to pay back the country with what he had learned so that he could live up to the Party's upbringing.

Luo Xibei (1926–2005), born in Xiangtan, Hunan Province, was a member of the Communist Party of China. He was the son of Luo Yinong, a leader of the early-stage Communist Party of China. He was a hydropower expert and former president of the Hydropower and Water Resources Planning and Design Institute.

Shortly after Luo's birth, his mother passed away in the Soviet Union due to drowning. His father sacrificed his life for the party in Shanghai in 1928. He became an orphan at the age of 2.

In 1954, Luo Xibei, who returned from the Moscow Power Engineering Institute of the Soviet Union, dived into the hydropower undertakings of New China. Faced with the blank in China's hydropower development, Luo Xibei was ready to sketch it with the latest and best picture. He went

Luo Xibei

deep into the gullies in the southwest, climbed hillsides, conducted a census, observed the drop, measured the water energy, and selected dam sites river by river. He investigated the entire Jinsha River three times, the Lancang River four times, and visited Guizhou Province seven times to develop the Wu River. His footprints were almost all over the 1023 km of the upper reaches of the Yellow River between Qinghai and Ningxia.

Luo Xibei had been engaged in hydropower planning, the survey, design, and construction technology work of hydraulic and hydropower engineering. He was a well-known expert in the kinetic energy economy and hydropower planning in China. He participated in the river planning and preliminary design of hydropower stations for the Longxi River and Dahong River. He took part in the survey, design and construction of large hydropower projects such as Liujia Gorge and Longyang Gorge. He also presided over and reviewed the feasibility study and preliminary design of a number of large and medium-sized hydropower projects such as Shuikou Dam, Lijia Gorge, Yantan Dam, and Manwan Dam. He organized and led the investigation and regulation of major rivers, including the upper reaches of the Yellow River, Wu River, and Lancang River. He provided suggestions for the Three Gorges Project and put forward the valuable opinion, "The main purpose of the Three Gorges Project is flood control, and power generation comes next." He advised constructing the two hydropower stations in the upper reaches, Xiluodu Dam and Xiangjiaba Dam, at the same time to alleviate the sediment deposition problem.

Liujiaxia Hydropower Station

For more than 50 years, Luo Xibei had made outstanding contributions to China's hydropower and hydraulic development. During the design and construction of Liujiaxia Hydropower Station, Luo Xibei and his team successfully first developed and promoted the new low fluid concrete technology as well as studied and adopted the new chemical grouting technology for the first time. The study "National Technical Policies in 12 Important Fields" he participated in in 1981 and the national general survey of water resources organized and led by him in 1985 won the first prize of the State's Science and Technology Advancement Award. His unique views on the reform of the hydropower economic system, such as the establishment of hydropower development companies by basins, were adopted and implemented by the central government and the State Council.

Luo Xibei actively advanced the development of pumped-storage power stations in China, joined and guided the evaluation and post-evaluation work of some hydraulic and hydropower projects, and put forward constructive suggestions on the layout, objectives, and implementation of hydropower development.

Luo Xibei had a solid theoretical foundation in hydraulics and was good at combining it with practice. He was the author of *River and Hydropower Economy*, *River Planning and Comprehensive Utilization of Water Resources*, *Water Resources Development Practice, and Regional Economy*, etc. These works were the crystallization of his decades of thought and experience in hydropower undertakings, which greatly influenced the hydraulic and hydropower in China and guided its development.

PAN JIAZHENG

Who Built the Three Gorges with His Dreams Rooted in Rivers

After the Japanese invaders occupied Hainan Island to plunder the iron ore resources, they built Dongfang Power Station for power generation in only two years. "The efficiency gained through plunder and cruelty was imaginably at the cost of quality." After Japan surrendered, the hydropower station was hit by severe floods, and the main equipment of the power station was destroyed and completely stopped functioning. Pan Jiazheng and his engineering team were assigned the task of repairing the station. When he entered the work shed, he surprisingly found many "suicide notes," enclosed word by word, the complaints of labor's blood and tears. "More than 3,000 laborers died of starvation, illness, or were even buried alive... Only about 200 people survived." These historical materials are so shocking, recalling his unforgettable memories.

In 1940, Shaoxing fell under the Japanese's occupation. The 13-year-old Pan Jiazheng was severely beaten because he did not bow to the Japanese sentries when passing the city gate. "The shame of being a colonial enslaved person was engraved in his heart since then. To wash away the shame, self-improvement is the only path. He said, "The country's demand is my ambition." Pan Jiazheng's heart burst out in the light of his belief in prospering the country with hydropower. This light guided him to work on rivers day and night, even till the last moment of his life.

PAN JIAZHENG (1927–2012), born in Shaoxing, Zhejiang Province, is a member of the Communist Party of China. He was an expert in hydraulic and hydropower engineering and civil engineering and an academician of the Chinese Academy of Sciences and the Chinese Academy of Engineering. He won the Guanghua Engineering Science and Technology Award and was a famous science fiction writer. He once served as the chairman of the Chinese National Commission on Large Dams, the head of the expert group for quality inspection of the Three

Pan Jiazheng

Gorges Project under the State Council, and the director of the Expert Committee of the South-North Water Diversion Project Construction Commission under the State Council. He was also a professor and doctoral supervisor at Tsinghua University.

In 1950, Pan Jiazheng graduated from the Department of Civil Engineering of Zhejiang University, becoming one of New China's first generation of hydropower professionals. Since he started his career at the Qiantang River Hydroelectric Power Survey Office in 1950, he had been progressing on the road of scientific research and engineering for more than half a century and has made great contributions to China's hydraulic and hydropower undertakings.

In 1954, Pan Jiazheng was transferred to the State's Administration of Beijing Hydroelectric Power and later served as technician, engineer, head engineer and deputy chief design engineer at Shanghai Hydropower Design Institute. In 1956, Pan Jiazheng presided over the design of Liuxihe thin arch dam, the first dam with flood discharge from dam crest in China and broke the ground for domestic development of thin arch dam. In 1957, Pan Jiazheng was appointed as the deputy chief engineer of Xin'anjiang Hydropower Station. He creatively transformed the original design of solid gravity dam into a slotted gravity dam. He initiated the pumping drainage theory, which adopted pumping

Three Gorges Project

and drainage measures to relieve the uplift pressure of the dam foundation and greatly reduced the engineering quantity of the dam. The completion of Xin'anjiang Hydropower Station set the first milestone of new China's hydropower undertakings. In contrast, Pan Jiazheng's innovative slotted gravity dam set an example for more than ten domestic dams including Danjiangkou and Panjiakou and become a widely adopted dam type in China.

Later, Pan Jiazheng participated in the design, planning, and scientific research of Beikou Tidal Power Station of Yangtze River, Huangpu River Tidal Gate, Shanxi and Jiuxi cascade power stations of Feiyun River, Qiantang River Tidal Power Station, Qililong hydropower station of Fuchun River and Hunanzhen hydropower station of Wuxijiang River. In 1965, he went to Yalong River to design Jinping Hydropower Station, opening the golden age of his design career. During this period, he created a number of "First in China" records: he presided over the design of China's first double-curvature thin arch dam, the first large-bottom-hole diversion dam, the first double-curvature high arch dam...

What made Pan renowned worldwide was the Three Gorges Project. He served as the deputy head and chief engineer of the Three Gorges Demonstration Leading Group. During ten more years from the beginning to the completion of the project, Pan Jiazheng took on the heavy responsibilities of technology, construction and quality, and served as the director of the Technical Committee of China Three Gorges Corporation. As the chief designer of the Three Gorges Dam, he made great contributions to the construction of the project.

ZHU BOFANG

Whose Path to Scientific Research Was Diligence

Zhu Bofang had a motto for study: work hard during the day and study hard at night. He took this motto as a lifestyle and persisted for nearly 70 years. How did Zhu Bofang make such outstanding achievements? He said that a fundamental point is to grasp one's work, which is to complete work with good quality, learn in the work and solve major and key technical problems. Zhu Bofang didn't live a legendary life, but he created miracles. He once summarized two sentences: First, "Start from production, think beyond production, apply in production." Second, "Be diligent in work, be diligent in learning, and be diligent in thinking."

ZHU BOFANG, born in Yujiang County, Jiangxi Province (now Yujiang District) in 1928, was an expert in hydraulic structure. He was an academician of Chinese Academy of Engineering and a senior engineer of China Institute of Water Resources and Hydropower Research.

Zhu Bofang studied at Shanghai Jiaotong University in his early years. He suspended his studies due to work and went to the site of Foziling for construction. From 1951 to 1956, Zhu Bofang participated in designing the first batch of three high dams (Foziling Dam, Meishan Dam and Xianghongdian Dam) in China, contributing to China's mastering of modern high dam design technologies and important innovations. At the Foziling site, his

Zhu Bofang

journey in technology and academia officially started. He had strong learning ability and was also full of great enthusiasm for learning. He mainly focused on the study of hydraulic structures. He initiated the division technology of dam concrete grade, saving huge amounts of investment. In 1957, he established a complete theoretical system of thermal creep stress and temperature control of hydraulic concrete, which solved the worldwide problem of "all dams crack." He initiated the digital model and solution of arch dam optimization, which can save 10%–30% of dam concrete. This method was applied to arch dams such as Xiaowan, Jinping, Xiluodu and other large-scale arch dams, saving more than two billion yuan in investment.

Zhu Bofang initiated the concrete dam simulation analysis method, which advanced the stress analysis level of concrete dam. He established the numerical monitoring method of concrete dam, which greatly improved the safety monitoring level of concrete dam. He developed the creep theory of concrete dam and proposed two creep theorems and a new creep stress analysis method. The research results were widely applied in actual projects and were included in the national codes for gravity dams, arch dams and hydraulic loads. The results of "Research on Temperature Stress of Hydraulic Concrete" won the third prize of National Award for Natural Sciences in 1982. The results of "Whole Process Simulation Analysis of Concrete High Dam and Research and Application of Temperature Stress" won the second prize of the State Science and Technology Advancement Award in 2000.

Zhu Bofang won one National Award for Natural Sciences, two State's Science and Technology Advancement Awards, a national-level title of National Science and Technology Expert with Outstanding Contribution, the Honor Award of International Commission on Large Dams and eight ministerial science and technology advancement awards. He carried out a large number of studies on dozens of hydropower stations including the Three Gorges, Xiaowan, Longtan, and Liujiaxi. The research results were widely applied, among which 14 have been adopted into China's dam engineering design code. He published ten monographs and 240 papers, making him one of the most productive scholars among dam experts of the same era. His work *Temperature Stress and Control of Mass Concrete* and *Principles and Application of Finite Element Method* was rated as one of the ten most popular works in civil engineering and hydropower major in China respectively, of which English versions were already published abroad.

Zhu Bofang was an expert in hydraulic structure and solid mechanics. He was widely recognized as the creator and founder of thermal stress, arch dam optimal design, and simulation of concrete dam in China. He enjoyed a high reputation in dam construction at home and abroad. He had abundant knowledge, went wide and deep in his research focuses, and made outstanding achievements in high dam design and dam construction technology. He was an authoritative scholar in the field of high arch dams in China.

Foziling Reservoir Dam

LIANG YINGCHEN
The "Builder" of Golden Gateway

He set feet on that land countless times feeling the ethos of the Three Gorges Reservoir Area. He once said, "the construction of the Three Gorges Project was a long-cherished dream for us, hydraulic professionals, for generations. When we were studying at university, we knew there was a TVA (Tennessee Valley Authority) in the United States, and now we also have a YVA (Yangtze Valley Authority). The Gezhouba Project is a part of the Three Gorges Project broadly speaking, and I was fortunate to participate in the construction of these two projects, and I feel very proud."

LIANG YINGCHEN (1928–2016), born in Baoding, Hebei Province, was a member of the Party of China. He was an expert in waterway and port engineering and an academician of the Chinese Academy of Engineering. He served as the director of the Leading Group Office of the Three Gorges Navigation Project of the Ministry of Transportation and Communications and the president of the Water Transport Planning and Design Institute of the Ministry of Transportation and Communications.

"To have enough food, you must plant land, which requires water and fertilizer." It was such idea that made Liang Yingchen, who was poor and hungry from a young age, set up the ambition to study water conservancy. In 1948, he chose the hydraulics team of the civil engineering department of Tsinghua University, thus forming an indissoluble bond with water conservancy and water transportation.

Liang Yingchen

In 1952, Liang Yingchen graduated from Tsinghua University early and was assigned to the Port of Tanggu in Tianjin, where he learned life-long experience and skills. Two years later, due to the urgent need of national construction, Liang Yingchen was assigned to the Soviet Union for a four-year term study on wave and seaport wharf structure. While studying abroad, he visited the ports along the Black Sea coast and broadened his vision, which laid a solid foundation for his later participation in port construction.

After returning to China in 1958, Liang Yingchen immediately devoted to the busy construction of New China and assisted with designing the Tanggu New Port Pier 3.

After the completion of the hydraulic project, one of its two major functions is flood control, the other was power generation and navigation. In 1971, Liang Yingchen began to take charge of the design of navigation structures of Gezhouba Dam. During the design and construction of Gezhouba, the project with the longest construction period, highest difficulty level and most complicated technologies he ever met, he overcame all kinds of difficulties, completed the overall design of the navigation lock, solved many complicated problems such as siltation, navigation flow conditions and the hydraulic structure and water conveyance system of the navigation lock. He accumulated abundant practical experience in the planning, scientific research and design of the navigation hub, and won the outstanding prize of the State's Science and Technology Advancement Award.

The construction of the Three Gorges Project was the beginning of Liang Yingchen's second encounter with the Yangtze River. Liang Yingchen participated in the navigation work of each stage of the Three Gorges Project, and contributed to the dam site selection, technical research, scientific demonstration, and solution of major key technical problems. He served as a

Navigation Lock of The Three Gorges Project

member of the Three Gorges Project Quality Inspection Expert Group of the Three Gorges Project Construction Committee of the State Council. He visited the construction site of the Three Gorges Project several times to inspect the construction quality of navigation structures. The navigation lock of the Three Gorges Project was one of the most complicated projects in its construction. It was the world's largest double-line five-grade navigation lock, with a total length of 6.4 km. Liang Yingchen and other experts collectively solved completely new technical problems of the key technologies of the Three Gorges project, such as the overall design of the large-scale navigation lock, the water conveyance of the ultra-high head navigation lock, and the large-scale lined navigation lock structure that co-acts with the high steep slope rock mass, five-grade navigation lock surveillance system and navigation lock construction.

Liang Yingchen devoted himself to the cause of water conservancy and navigation his entire life, participated in and led the planning, design, feasibility studies and review of a number of large and medium-sized ports and channels, and contributed lifelong talents and painstaking efforts. He has particularly made significant contributions in developing Three Gorges's navigation.

WANG SANYI

Who Always Kept Dam Safety in Mind

Wang Sanyi served as the study director of the Student Union during his study in the Civil Engineering Department of Tangshan Engineering College. He took the initiative to demand progress and joined the Communist Youth League in 1951. In 1952, when he was still a sophomore, he responded to the call of the Party and the motherland to "resist the U.S. and aid Korea to protect the homeland." He resolutely participated in the Chinese People's Volunteer Air Force to fight in North Korea. He repaired the airport and other facilities under the constant bombing of enemy aircraft and was awarded merit citation of second class.

Wang was very concerned about the cultivation and education of young intellectuals. Once, he told them, "China's development had taken many wrong paths and finally welcomed today's glorious era. In human history, technology and economy had never developed as fast with such charm. You are in such a good era for development, of which projects are so much better than the project scale and conditions I worked on when I first came to China South Institute. In such a good era, you can give full play to your talents and make great achievements. You must cherish the time, study hard, work hard on the construction site, complete more practical work, research deeply, and think frequently to train yourselves in practice."

WANG SANYI (1929–2003), born in Tonglu, Zhejiang Province, was a member of the Communist Party of China. He was an expert in hydraulic structure design, and an academician of the Chinese Academy of Engineering. He was born into a scholarly family in Tonglu, Zhejiang Province. His parents taught him by percept and examples which influenced Wang Sanyi since childhood. He understood that he has to study well to develop his motherland with his knowledge after he grows up.

In 1948, Wang Sanyi was admitted to the Hydraulic Engineering major of the Department of Civil Engineering of Tangshan Engineering College. During his study, he joined the Chinese People's Volunteers Army to fight in North Korea. After returning to China, he devoted himself to developing his motherland with great enthusiasm immediately after

Wang Sanyi

finishing off his military services. China's water conservancy undertakings needed talents, so he transferred from the department of civil engineering to the department of hydraulic engineering to study, starting his lifelong relationship with hydraulics and hydropower.

In the early days after the founding of the People's Republic of China, although the construction condition was difficult, it didn't constrain the great enthusiasm of Wang Sanyi in developing the motherland. He left his footprints all over the mountains and rivers in Jiangxi, Hubei, Guizhou and other provinces. He withstood the hardship and collected precious first-hand survey one after another. Wang Sanyi was good at learning, always solved problems with cross-disciplinary thinking, and applied it to the design of hydropower station as guidance. He emphasized that project designer must grasp the first-hand information thoroughly. In order to obtain practical and reliable field data, he often went back and forth between various hydropower sites, climbing high mountains, exploring dangerous caves, even including those as small as underground river holes of only few cubic meters. He said, "No matter how deep, narrow or dangerous these caves are, you have to go inside and see them clearly." He often climbed up cliff steep over 70 degrees with the geologists, and personally knocked all stones found in excavation with the geological hammer piece by piece meticulously.

In his hydropower career of more than 50 years, Wang Sanyi has designed many high dams and large hydropower stations, presided over, and participated in the survey and design of more than 40 hydropower stations such as Wujiangdu, Longtan, Dongjiang, Wuqiangxi and Bailianhe. From Hubei to Guizhou Province, granite to limestone, Wang Sanyi had been constantly studying high dam design and complex foundation treatment. He rigorously demonstrated, took challenges, and solved difficult problems with his colleagues in the dangerous karst area, which paved the way for tackling technical problems in building high dams in limestone areas of China.

Wang Sanyi presided over the Wujiangdu Hydropower Station dam design, which was the highest dam built in China's strong karst area in the 1970s. After years of operation, the leakage was extremely small, creating a miracle. In connection with the extremely complex terrain and geological conditions of the dam site, the project adopted arch gravity dam with lower arch and upper gravity, a powerhouse top with high water head and large unit-width flow, flood discharge in front of the powerhouse, and several innova-

Wujiangdu Dam

tive design including the powerhouse behind the dam, spillway, and overlapping layout of the switch station in the narrow river valley. As the technical director of the project design, Wang Sanyi won the first prize of the State's Science and Technology Advancement Award in 1985. He led the design of projects such as Dongjiang Dam and Wuqiangxi dam (both won the National Design Gold Award), Daguangba Dam, Wulichong Dam and other projects had many technical innovations. Wang Sanyi has made outstanding contributions to the development of hydropower construction and the economy in China. He was awarded the title "Chinese Engineering Design Master" in 1994.

LIU GUANGRUN

Who Benefited the Three Gorges with His Ability to Realize Its Unreleased Potential

Liu Guangrun, at the age of 29, dared to challenge foreign experts on their "conclusion" of the selected site location of the Three Gorges Project. He had grasped many scientific field data. More importantly, for him the benefit of his motherland was the utmost among all. He attached his entire life to the Three Gorges, and once wrote: The Great River then turned east, breaking Wushan Mountain like an axe. But the water was still full of energy, flooding Wu and Chu. The disaster must be stopped and the energy must be used, to benefit the Three Gorges and around.

LIU GUANGRUN (1929–2007), was from Baodi County (now Baodi District, Tianjin), Hebei Province. He was a member of the Communist Party of China, a famous expert in hydrogeology and engineering geology, and an academician of the Chinese Academy of Engineering. He was also a professor of Huazhong University of Science and Technology, a visiting professor of China University of Geosciences, and a visiting researcher of the Chinese Academy of Geological Sciences.

Liu Guangrun graduated from Nanjing Geological Prospecting Specialized School in 1952. After graduation, he was assigned to the Engineering Geological Survey Team of the Yellow River Basin Planning of the Ministry of Geology and participated in the geological survey of the reach between Baotou and Yumenkou and the dam sites of Wanjiazhai

Liu Guangrun

and Longkou. From 1955 to 1957, Liu Guangrun went overseas to study hydraulic engineering geology in the Hydropower Academy of the Soviet Union. After he returned to China, he was assigned to the Three Gorges Project Geological Brigade of the Ministry of Geology as the technical director due to his excellent grade.

On the site selection of the Three Gorges Project, Liu Guangrun led the project technicians to carry out a large number of field investigations. In conjunction with the investigation results, he believed that Nanjinguan, which was selected as Three Gorges Dam's site location by Savage, the Chief Design Engineer of the U.S. Bureau of Reclamation, was not a good fit. Limestone karsts in Nanjinguan was strongly developed with many underground cavities, while Sandouping was of igneous granite stratum with solid, stable, and complete weathered layer. As the technical director of the geological exploration of the Three Gorges Project, he made great contributions to the correct selection of the Sandouping dam's site location.

In the 1980s and 1990s, Liu Guangrun was appointed as the head of the expert group for the technical research of Three Gorges, "A study on the major geological and seismic problems of the Three Gorges Project." He guided technicians to complete major special studies on the crustal stability of the dam area, the stability of the reservoir bank slope and the reservoir-induced earthquake, which provided important scientific basis for the decision-making and design optimization of the Three Gorges Project.

In 1985, a major landslide occurred along the reach between Guangjiayan and Xintan Town of the Yangtze River, which destroyed Xintan Town and cut off the navigation of the Yangtze River. Just two years ago, experts such as Liu Guangrun predicted the risk of landslide in the area and suggested to relocate Xintan Town. Their scientific prediction, timely mobilization, and accurate forecast of the relevant departments protected the 457 households and 1371 residents who lived in this large landslide risk area from casualties. After the landslide occurred, Liu Guangrun carefully surveyed the landslide area and observed the deformation of the landslide towards the Yangtze River with a bamboo pole in hand at the risk of his life. He also made the judgment that navigation of the Yangtze River could be restored, which avoided more economic losses.

In 2003, the first phase of the Three Gorges Dam was about to store water for power generation. The State's Council established a leading group to prevent and regulate geological disasters in the Three Gorges Reservoir of the Yangtze River. Liu Guangrun was appointed as the head of the expert group. He organized various relevant demonstrations on the prevention and regulation of geological disasters in the Three Gorges Reservoir Area and proposed many plans.

From the safety of the Three Gorges navigation channel, the safety of the reservoir area to the safety of the middle and lower reaches, Liu Guangrun had always been concerned about the hazards that geological disasters bring to the local area and residents' lives. The significance of people's life was above all else. He once said that he needs to be accountable to the Party and the people. He was known as the "Scout" and "The Guadian of the Three Gorges" of the Three Gorges Project due to his engagement in the geological disaster regulation of the Three Gorges Project and the reservoir storage security and relocation project which ensured the safety of the people. His research achievements won the first prize of the State Science and Technology Advancement Award and National Excellent Science and Technology Book Award, two ministerial science and technology advancement awards. He was also awarded the honorary titles of "Li Siguang Geological Science Award" and "Geological Professional with Significant Contribution." As the main recommender of Sandouping as Three Gorges Project's dam site, his contribution will be forever engraved in future generations' minds.

CHEN MINGZHI

The "Rider of Waves and Tides" Whose Contribution Was Countrywide

Chen Mingzhi believed that "invigorating China through science and education" was a strategy that conforms to the national conditions and the people's will. He exhausted all his efforts to promote the implementation of this national strategy with the development of water conservancy undertakings. As an academician of the Chinese Academy of Engineering, he had always advocated that China's water conservancy should follow the road of reform, innovation, development and support the national development with water conservancy to ensure the safety of people's water resources. He always put the interests of his country and people in his heart.

CHEN MINGZHI (1929–2008), born in Fuzhou, Fujian Province, was a member of the Communist Party of China. He was an expert in hydraulic engineering, dam engineering, and an academician of the Chinese Academy of Engineering. He was also the former chief engineer of Songliao River Water Resources Committee of the Ministry of Water Resources.

Chen Mingzhi

In 1950, Chen Mingzhi graduated from Shanghai Jiaotong University. At that time, he could have stayed in Shanghai. Still, he abandoned his superior working and living conditions in Shanghai and left for devoting to the development of Northeast China where ruins were waiting for restoration. In July of the same year, he became a technician in the General Administration of Water Resources of Northeast China People's Government.

For over 50 years, Chen Mingzhi was mainly engaged in the planning, design and technical leadership of hydraulic and hydropower projects. He participated in or presided over the design and review of more than 50 hydraulic and hydropower projects, including Dahuofang Reservoir, Qinghe Reservoir, Taipingwan Reservoir in Liaoning Province, Fengman Hydropower Station in Jilin Province, and Datengxia Water Conservancy Hydropower Project in Guangxi Province. During the design and construction process of Dahuofang Reservoir, he initiated earth dam stability analysis and a new method of tunnel lining design. Through investigation and experiments, he proposed to widen the earth dam trench from 6m to 15m combined with cement grouting. The test was successful and promoted. In the 1970s, he organized and led the design of Baishan Hydropower Station. By adopting a series of technologies such as three-centered gravity arch dam and air slot on the dam surface, the project's engineering quantities was reduced, avoided cavitation, and was prevented from the sliding of fault fracture zone. He also participated in the scheme research and demonstration of reinforcement scheme of more than 20 hydropower projects in more than ten provinces, such as Danjiangkou Dam in Hubei Province, Panjiakou Dam, Yuecheng Reservoir in

Hebei Province, Cetian Reservoir in Shanxi Province, Tianshengqiao-I Dam in Guizhou Province, and Jilintai I Dam in Xinjiang.

In 1995, he participated in the South-North Water Diversion Project demonstration and acted as the line team leader. Since 1996, he served as the technical committee director for the construction of Xiaolangdi Dam of the Yellow River. From 1974 to 1976, he participated in designing and reviewing hydropower stations in five African countries.

In 1983, Chen Mingzhi established Songliao River Water Resources Commission. From 1984 to 1993, he presided over the compilation of the *Plan of Comprehensive Development and Utilization of Water Resources in the Songhua River and Liao River Basin* and served as the coordination group head. The State Council approved the plan for implementation in 1994.

Baishan Hydropower Station

Chen Mingzhi dedicated himself to rivers his whole life. He has made great contributions to China's water conservancy, especially to the hydraulic and hydropower construction in Northeast China.

LIN GAO

The Groundbreaker for the Discipline of Earthquake-resistant Dam

Lin Gao always dreamed of making China a country that not only builds dams in high quantity, but also with great quality. In 2008, after hearing the news of the Wenchuan earthquake, Lin Gao could barely eat and sleep and was particularly concerned about the safety of Zipingpu reservoir dam. He said, "At that time, the situation was like a large basin of water had been put over the heads of Chengdu residents. Once the dam cracks down, it would be a disaster." Although he was already 79 years old, he insisted on investigating on site. In the time of crisis, Lin Gao thought, "The demand of the nation is our guide for action." All of the dams he worked on were a epitome of his climb to the higher level of science. While the country was developing, he was also constantly expanding new research focuses. His relentless pursuit of scientific research to serve the country's needs has never stopped.

LIN GAO was born in Nanchang, Jiangxi Province in 1929. He was a member of the Communist Party of China, an expert in hydraulic engineering and seismic engineering, and an academician of the Chinese Academy of Sciences. He served as a director and professor of the Vibration and Strength Testing Center of Dalian University of Technology.

Lin Gao graduated from the Department of Civil Engineering of Tsinghua University in 1951 and the Water Resources Utilization Seminar of Dalian Engineering Institute (now Dalian Institute of Technology) in 1954, after

Lin Gao

which he stayed in the university to work. In 1981, he was elected as the first batch of doctoral supervisors of hydraulic structure major in China and cultivated many talents in the industry. Many of his students became leading figures in the industry, academic leaders or key technical personnel of their institutes.

In addition to teaching, he had also been engaging in the scientific research in the field of hydraulic structure engineering for a long time. He made important contributions in aspects such as the theory and model experiment technology of dam and the theoretical research of underground structure seismic analysis and the concrete structure dynamic fracture technology. He played an important role in solving seismic issues, the key technical field of dam, seaport, nuclear power station, etc.

Lin Gao was one of China's major founders of dam seismic discipline. He took the lead in carrying out the first vibration test of arch dam in China. He conducted scientific research on seismic test technology of earth-rock dam, which solved the key technical problems of large-scale earthquake-resistant engineering structure. In 1956, the arch dam of Liuxi River in Guangdong Province adopted the scheme of dam crest trajectory bucket for flood discharge. Dalian University of Technology undertook the test and research work. Lin Gaoyong, who just launched his career, took over the heavy responsibility and presided over the test. The first arch dam vibration test in China was completed in just over one year. It demonstrated the feasibility of the scheme of dam crest trajectory bucket for flow discharge, which provided strong technical support for the design. In 1958, the seismic technology of earth-rock fill dam in China was basically undeveloped. During the construction of Yilihe Earth Dam Project in the meizoseismal area of Yunnan Province, Lin Gao and the team carried out the longitudinal bending earthquake-resistant stability test of the first buttress dam model in China. They proposed the seismic response calculation model of arch dam and gravity dam. The results of this study eventually provided proper seismic safety evaluation of the project, and the proposed seismic measures were adopted by the construction contractors. In 1978, although lacking laboratory instruments and equipment, Lin Gao carried out the seismic test of Baishan arch dam, the highest arch dam in China at that time, through self-developed direct photography method. The test obtained the arch dam's first nine modes of vibration with positive and negative symmetry. In 1985, Lin Gao was entrusted with the mission to work out a dynamic response calculation program for analysis and calculation at the difficult moment. His research results on resisting the safety issues of rock plug blasting of Fengman Dam won the first prize of the State Science and Technology Advancement Award.

Lin Gao was responsible for several national scientific and technological research projects in the Sixth, Seventh, Eighth, and Ninth Five-Year Plan, as well as key projects of the National Natural Science Foundation of China, which improved the research level of seismic technology for dams in China. He has also made innovative achievements in areas such as the dynamic characteristics of concrete materials, the dynamic interaction between structure and fluid, and the dynamic interaction between structure and infinite foundation.

Fengman Dam

Lin Gao had been deeply engaging in the field of dam seismic research with dedicated research, which has improved the level of dam seismic design and safety evaluation in China, advancing the dam seismic research in China to a leading international level.

QIU DAHONG

A Loyalist of the Sea Who Was Raised in South of the Lower Reaches of the Yangtze River

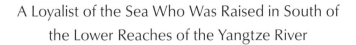

As a child, Qiu Dahong witnessed the Japanese invaders wantonly burning, killing and looting China, which resulted in his strong desire to save the country through science. In 1947, Qiu Dahong was admitted to the Department of Civil Engineering of Tsinghua University. At the beginning of 1949, when Beiping was liberated, Qiu Dahong, a sophomore, followed the People's Liberation Army for promotion in town. For the first time in his life, he truly saw the real life of the toiling people, which strengthened his life belief to go to where the motherland needed the most. Upon graduation, Qiu Dahong resolutely gave up the opportunity to stay in school as a teacher and responded to New China's call of "go to the front line of industrial development, go to the northeast." He came to Dalian Institute of Technology, a new university founded by the Communist Party of China.

QIU DAHONG, whose family was from Wuxing, Zhejiang Province (now Nanxun Town in Huzhou City), was born in Shanghai in 1930. He was an expert in coastal and offshore engineering, and a pioneer and educator in the coastal and offshore engineering discipline. He was also an academician of the Chinese Academy of Sciences and a professor of Dalian University of Technology.

Qiu Dahong

In 1951, Qiu Dahong graduated from the Department of Civil Engineering of Tsinghua University. He responded to the national call and came to Dalian Engineering Institute (now Dalian University of Technology), starting his career as a teacher. He had been teaching for more than 70 years and had students all over the world. As the first institution in China that set up seaport engineering major, Dalian Institute of Technology has trained the earliest batch of experts and scholars in seaport, most of whom were students of Qiu Dahong. During his teaching career, he undertook the teaching tasks of many fundamental and specialized courses such as port and port engineering buildings, engineering hydrology, wave theory, etc.

Qiu Dahong insisted on combining teaching, production, scientific research, and carried out innovative research in shallow sea waves, wave forces, and irregular waves. At a young age, he was brave enough to take over the heavy burden to lead research independently. In 1958, he served as the general director of the Dalian Fishing Port Technical Project, which was the largest in Asia at that time. In 1973, he served as the main technical director of Port of Dalian, China's first modern crude oil export port. He presided over the design of the model, overall and detailed structure of the wharf, and served as the design representative of the construction site. The design and research of this project won the National Science Conference Award and the National Design Excellence Gold Award of the State's Construction Commission in the

1970s. In 1983, he served as the head and the general technical director of the joint design team of oil resources for the development of Beibu Gulf in the South China Sea.

Qiu Dahong mainly engaged in the research and technical work of application foundation and engineering design in coastal, port, and offshore engineering. He developed the engineering application theory and experimental verification of nonlinear elliptic cosine wave in shallow water area, summarized the practical calculation method of the force of irregular wave and elliptic cosine wave on common marine structures, and systematically studied the interaction between wave seepage in the seabed and marine structures. The research results provided more practical scientific basis for coastal engineering design.

Dalian Fishing Port

Qiu Dahong also successively participated in the model test, design, scientific and technological consulting and advising work of Port of Qinhuangdao, Navy Floating Dock, Container Terminal of Port of Lianyungang, Container and Bulk Grain Terminal of Shenzhen Chiwan Port, Hainan Oil Terminal, Yamen Channel Project of the Pearl River in Guangdong, Yangshan Deepwater Port Area of Shanghai Port, Yangtze River Estuary Deepwater Channel Project, Caofeidian Reclamation Project in Tangshan, Hebei Province, Oujiang Estuary Regulation Project in Wenzhou, Zhejiang Province, Yangpu Port in Hainan Province, and other projects.

Taking root in Northeast China along the coast, Qiu Dahong has made great contributions to fields including wharf, oil port, and waterway engineering and technologies.

LU YAORU

The Geologist Who Diligently Pursued His Goal

2019 was a special year for Lu Yaoru. He said, "I am 88 years old this year, which is the 66th anniversary of my Communist Party of China membership, the 66th anniversary of my career and the 70th anniversary of my study of geology." With this timing, he chose to donate his personal assets of 3.6 million yuan. He set up "Lu Yaoru Ecological Environment and Geological Engineering Incentive Fund" under the Tongji University Education Development Foundation to support and promote the development of ecological environment and geological engineering relevant disciplines to become world-class disciplines as well as support the talent training, transformation of scientific research, and achievement of these disciplines. At the donation ceremony, he wrote a poem: "Spring sun is shining and my emotion is surging. I would express myself by modifying a poem by Li Shangyin. Till the end of life, a silk worm keeps spining silk. Till burning itself out, a candle goes on lighting us. It is my responsibility to contribute my whole life to my country. And to benefit my people even afterlife. It is now the best time of the age, and I would keep chasing my dream in the remainder of my life."

In 1931, Lu Yaoru was born in Fuzhou, Fujian Province. He was a member of the Communist Party of China, an expert in engineering geology, hydrogeology, and environmental geology, and an academician of the Chinese Academy of Engineering. He was also a professor and doctoral supervisor of Tongji University.

Lu Yaoru was admitted to the Department of Geology of Tsinghua University in 1950. She started the cross-disciplinary study between geology, hydraulics and civil engineering under the background of national development at that time. After the college adjustment in 1952, he joined Beijing Geology Institute and studied from foreign experts. He graduated early in 1953 and joined the Communist Party of China in the same year.

After graduation, Lu Yaoru started his career as a member of the

Lu Yaoru

geological brigade. He began to engage in hydrogeological surveys from northeast China to Xin'anjiang, singing the *Song of the Investigation Team Members* along the way. From 1954 to 1956, he was responsible for investigating the reservoir in Qixian County. From 1956 to 1957, he participated in the investigation of Guanting Reservoir. From 1961 to 1963, he worked in the hydrogeological engineering geological research team of the Longmen Hydropower Project of the Yellow River. From 1978 to 1990, he participated in solving the karst problems during the construction of high dams and hydro power stations like Wujiangdu and Dongfeng. Lu Yaoru had been engaging in the practice and research of karst and related hydrogeology, engineering geology and environmental geology for a long time. He established the theory of karst development and engineering environmental effect system. He participated in the practice and guidance of the investigation and research of hydraulic and hydropower projects, railway, mine and urban projects. In Huai River, Xin'an River, Hai River, Changjiang River, the Yellow River, the Pearl River and other basins, he led and guided the investigation and research of more than 100 large and medium-sized hydraulic and hydropower projects, such as Guanting, Xin'an River, Three Gorges (limestone dam area), Wujiangdu, etc. He also carried out investigation, research and guidance task for mining, railway, airport, wharf, and urban and rural development. He devoted himself to prevent and control geological disasters and established a new theory of geological ecological environment, which advanced the poverty alleviation and sustainable development of southwest China and provided the basis for decision-making for preventing disasters and benefiting development.

In 1954, Lu Yaoru was responsible for investigating karst seepage and comparing schemes of the Xin'an River reservoir area. In 1956, he took charge of studying the seepage and collapse issues of Guanting reservoir dam, which posed a threat to Beijing and Tianjin. He was then responsible for the investigation and research of comparing the carbonate dam area for the Three Gorges Project (including the dam line selected by American engineer Savage). He paid most of his efforts to these three projects. While working on the Xin'an River Reservoir, he confirmed that there

Guanting Reservoir

was no major karst leakage problem in Xin'anjiang Reservoir area and first-grade development of high dam is better than multi-grade development. During the construction of Guanting Reservoir, he reported the causes of reservoir leakage and collapse. He put forward the treatment plan, which relieved the risk of great threat to Beijing and Tianjin in case of dam collapse and protected the the city's and people's safety. His work was recognized in the investigation of the dam site of Three Gorges Project.

In the early 1960s, Lu Yaoru presided over establishing the first Karst Research Office in China and established the Karst Geological Institute. He served as a senior expert in China's foreign-aid large-scale hydraulic projects, presided over the first international academic conference on sustainable development in karst areas, and won the National Science Conference Award, Geological Science and Technology Award, National Book Award for Outstanding Scientific and Technological Book and Li Siguang Geological Science Award. Because of his outstanding achievements in karst research, scholars at home and abroad praised him as Karst Lu.

DOU GUOREN

An Expert in Sediment Who Solved Many Siltation Problems

As the students who were to pursue studies in the Soviet Union, Dou Guoren and his classmates were received by Liu Shaoqi and Zhou Enlai before departure. Liu Shaoqi said, "The country's current task is development, requiring talents. Our country's financial condition is still quite difficult. It's an investment for us to spend a lot of money to send you abroad for studies. Your task is to help develop the country when you return from your studies. You have a long way to go with heavy responsibilities on your shoulder. The living expenses and tuition fees of each of you are at the cost of the production of 17 workers and peasants, and you should cherish this opportunity." These words were deeply imprinted in Dou Guoren's heart, he felt the great duty put on his shoulders. Although he was the youngest of the overseas students, he studied particularly hard and eventually earned a doctorate in technological science. Once, when his friends gathered together to watch a movie about China, one Soviet friend mocked the scene that showed China's underdevelopment during their chat. Dou Guoren tried hard to argue with him and defend China. Dou Guoren once said that true patriotism is to be patriotic everywhere, especially abroad.

Dou Guoren

DOU GUOREN (1932–2001), born in Beizhen, Liaoning Province, was a member of the Communist Party of China. He was an expert in sediment and river dynamics, an academician of the Chinese Academy of Sciences, and an honorary president and senior engineer of Nanjing Hydraulic Research Institute.

In 1951, Dou Guoren was admitted to the Department of Electrical Engineering of Tsinghua University, and then went to study port channel at the Department of Hydraulic Engineering of Leningrad Institute of Water Transport in the Soviet Union. While studying in the Soviet Union, he worked hard and received his doctor's degree in 1959. In 1960, at the age of 28, he received his Ph.D. in technical science, becoming one of the few outstanding students among the international students in Soviet Union. In the same year, he returned from the Soviet Union to work in Nanjing Hydraulic Research Institute, where he mainly engaged in the research on the basic theory of river sediment and sediment movement and put forward high-level insights on solving sedimentation in Qiantang River and Yangtze River Estuary. He derived the equation of unbalanced sediment transport of unsteady flow. He proposed the calculation method of sediment incipient velocity, unified formula of sedimentation, unified riverbed form equation of alluvial plain river and tidal estuary, and other important research results, which was widely applied in other engineering practices.

In the 1970s, Dou Guoren, together with other comrades, undertook the task of sediment deposition in the Gezhouba Project. He devoted himself to studying physical model test theory of sediment and established the physical model test theory of full sediment, which was successfully applied in the project.

The total sediment physical model became an effective approach to solve the sediment problem of major water hydraulic projects. This research result was awarded the outstanding prize in the State Science and Technology Advancement Award in 1985 titled "Research on Gezhouba Er Jiang, San Jiang Project and Hydroelectric Generating Unit."

In the 1980s, Dou Guoren studied the stochastic theory of riverbed, comprehensively and systematically expounded the pulsed structure, time-averaged structure and resistance law of turbulence and drag reduction in riverbed, and theoretically derived the eigenvalue and the spectral function formula of each pulse. The study formed a stochastic theory of riverbed turbulence, composed of three parts: turbulence stochastic model, wall detour flow mechanism, and turbulence probability. The study won the second prize of the National Award for Natural Sciences in 1987.

In the late 1980s, Dou Guoren participated in the study of the sediment problem of the Three Gorges Project. As the deputy group head of the sediment team of the demonstration stage of the Three Gorges Project, he solved the problem of sediment deposition in the feasibility demonstration of the Three Gorges Project. He also solved the key technical problems of the physical model of sediment in the long river section of the fluctuating backwater area from theoretical and practical perspectives. He developed the two-dimensional total sediment mathematical model of the river channel and established the world's longest (800 m) river channel sediment model. He studied the sediment deposition of the scheme of each water level of the Three Gorges Project and its impact on navigation, the results of which won the first prize of the Science and Technology Advancement Award awarded of the Ministry of Transportation and Communications in 1989.

In the 1990s, Dou Guoren carried out the study on the sediment problem of Xiaolangdi Reservoir in the Yellow River, established the sediment transport formula of hyperconcentrated flow and its model similarity law, conducted research on the sediment problem of the estuary under the action of waves and the coaction of wave and tidal current, and developed the mathematical model of estuary and coast sediment under the coaction of wave and tidal current. During the regulation of Huanghua Port and deep-water channel regulation of the Yangtze River Estuary, his research on siltation provided scientific basis for the completion of both projects. Dou Guoren dedicated his whole life to the cause of water conservancy and water transportation in China and made outstanding contributions to develop Nanjing Hydraulic Research Institute into a first-class research institute.

MAO ZHI

The Pioneer in Water-saving Irrigation

During the Anti-Japanese War, Mao Zhi encountered torrents and river floods many times in Sichuan. He witnessed the miserable situation of land submergence, house destruction and displacement of victims. All this left a deep mark on his young heart. Since then, he made up his mind to choose hydraulic engineering major in the future, so that he could learn how to regulate water, prevent disasters, and benefit the people.

MAO ZHI was born in Nanjing, Jiangsu Province in 1932. He was a member of the Communist Party of China, an irrigation and water conservancy expert, and an academician of the Chinese Academy of Engineering. He was also a professor and doctoral supervisor of Wuhan University. He served as an advisor to the Science and Technology Committee of the Ministry of Water Resources and a director of the Engineering Technology Committee of the National Water-saving Irrigation Engineering Technology Center (Beijing).

Mao Zhi

In 1953, Mao Zhi graduated from East China Institute of Water Conservancy (now Hohai University). He graduated one year early because the First Five-Year Plan of China was just officially implemented at that time, and the country urgently needed a large number of scientific and technological talents to support socialist construction. When he was filling out the graduation assignment application form, he wrote only six words: North China, Northeast China and Northwest China. He actively responded to the national call and went to teach at the Department of Water Resources of Hebei Agricultural College.

In 1955, due to the national college adjustments, Mao Zhi was transferred to Wuhan Institute of Water Conservancy (now Wuhan University) to teach in the Department of Farmland Water Resources. Over the years, he has made many achievements in the teaching, scientific research, and publication of farmland irrigation especially in the theory and technology of irrigation engineering and its water use management. He put forward advanced and practical theory and method of real-time forecast of water demand and irrigation as well as a water-saving irrigation mode with high yield of rice. He was the first person who put forward the law of spatio-temporal variation law of water production function and theory of crop growth "rebound" due to rehydration after drought, and the method of guiding water-saving irrigation with such theories, which proposed advanced and practical water-saving theory and technology for the operation, planning, design and the development and utilization of water resources of irrigation projects.

In the 1950s, Mao Zhi was the first to put forward a method to calculate crop water demand based on water vapor diffusion principle. Based on the principle of water vapor diffusion, he proposed a method to calculate rice water demand by stages using sunshine, air temperature, wind speed, and cultivation level as indexes, which was one of the earliest semi-empirical methods to calculate the water demand according to the cause theory in China.

Since 1980s, Mao Zhi studied the law of crop water demand under water-saving condition and put forward the real-time forecast method of crop water demand and irrigation. This method improved the water-saving and high yield of crops. It was highly praised by the FAO and the International Commission on Irrigation and Drainage at that time and was identified as "international advanced level." In 1995, it won the second prize of Science and Technology Advancement Award of the Ministry of Water Resources.

In the 1990s, Mao Zhi presided over the project of "Research on Rice Water Production Function and Rice Field Insufficient Irrigation Principle." He was the first to find a close relationship between the water function of rice and water demand of reference crops, which is the comprehensive meteorological index reflecting the atmospheric dry and wet level. He put forward the relevant mathematical model and developed the theory and method of exploring and analyzing the spatio-temporal

Water-saving irrigation

variation law of the crop water production function according to the model. In terms of water-saving mechanism, he proposed that the growth and water consumption of crops will have "rebound effect" with crops rehydration after mild and moderate drought in the early and middle stages of its growth. He also put forward the "rebound effect" method to guide the water-saving irrigation and insufficient irrigation, which explored new paths for guiding the water-saving farmland irrigation. His research achievements on water-saving irrigation were applied and promoted in many provinces and cities, which created enormous benefits and improved the sustainable and reasonable utilization of water resources and the development of economy and society.

CHEN HOUQUN

Who Chased His Dreams on the Dams

"I am willing to go anywhere as long as the motherland needs me there." Chen Houqun said, "I am now 90 years old, looking back on my past years, I'd like to call my life a dream life. Ever since my youth, the prosperity of my motherland has been my long-cherished wish. I am ready to take off whenever the country needs me."

CHEN HOUQUN, born in Wuxi, Jiangsu Province in 1932, was a member of the Communist Party of China. He was an expert in hydraulic structures, an academician of the Chinese Academy of Engineering. He once served as senior engineer and director of the Aseismic Engineering Research Center of China Institute of Water Resources and Hydropower Research Institute.

In March 1950, Chen Houqun started studying in the Civil Engineering Department of Tsinghua University. In January 1956, Chen Houqun joined the Communist Party

Chen Houqun

of China and won the title of "Excellent Communist Party Member" many times. In February 1958, Chen Houqun returned to China after graduation from the Moscow Power Engineering Institute of the Soviet Union and worked in the China Institute of Water Resources and Hydropower Research Institute as the head of the professional team, thus launching his career in water conservancy.

Chen Houqun successively presided over and completed the structural aseismic research of Liujiaxia Dam, Xinfengjiang Dam, Fengshuba Dam, Baishan Dam, Ertan Dam, Dongjiang Dam, Xiaolangdi Dam, Laxiwa, Xiaowan Dam, Three Gorges Projext, Xiluodu Dam and other large-scale projects as key personnel, providing scientific basis for solving major engineering problems, and obtaining certain social and economic benefits. Considering the complexity of seismic problems in major projects, Chen Houqun paid attention to the test and field observation of analysis and calculation. In the early 1980s, he was responsible for constructing the first large-scale three-dimensional six-degree-of-freedom simulated seismic shaking table in China, which was rated as the "world's best seismic test equipment for dam construction" by his peers at home and abroad. He carried out aseismic verification for the structures and equipment of the Three Gorges Project, Qinshan Nuclear Power Plant, large oil tank, Beijing TV Tower, and other major projects.

Chen Houqun edited the first publication of the national standard of hydraulic earthquake-resistant design, *Code for Seismic Design of Hydraulic Structures*, which filled in the blank of China's hydraulic aseismic design standard. He established the aseismic engineering research center and researched "300 m High Arch Dam Aseismic Technical Problems," a national key scientific and technological research project of the "Nineth Five-Year Plan" as the project leader. His project "Research on Dongjiang Arch Dam Reservoir Water Foundation Dynamic Interaction Field Test" was awarded the second prize of the State's Science and Technology Advancement Award. His research on high-performance parallel "cloud computing" dam aseismic analysis software was awarded the Tianhe Excellence in Application Innovation Award. In the Three Gorges Project, he participated in various research work many times. In 2005, he participated in the aseismic design research of the rack-climbing type ship lift of the Three Gorges Project. In 2008, he served as the deputy head of the seismology and geology group in the "Periodic Evaluation Report on Experimental Water Storage of the Three Gorges Project." The research on aseismic safety of high arch dams in the west made great achievements, guaranteeing the safe operation of high arch dams and large reservoirs.

Chen Houqun successively won the titles of "Young and Middle-aged Experts Nationally Acknowledged with Their Outstanding Contributions," "Outstanding Model Workers of the National Water Conservancy System," "National Advanced Producers" and "National May 1st Labour Medal." He won the Science and Technology Advancement Award of He-Liang-He-Li Fund in 2001, the Guanghua Engineering Science and Technology Award in 2009, and the International Large Dam Commission Lifetime Achievement Award in 2011.

Dong River Arch Dam

After being elected as an academician, he took on the heavy responsibility and served as the director of the expert committee of the South-North Water Diversion Project Construction Committee. He led the expert team to visit the project site for quality inspection and technical guidance in order to provide successful consultation for project's construction. In 2012, he also served as the head of the quality inspection expert group of the Three Gorges Project. He led the team to visit the site dozens of times to ensure the safe and efficient construction and operation of the Three Gorges Project. His proposal of aseismic design of the Three Gorges ship lift saved the country billions of yuan in cost. In 2020, he was awarded the title "Most Beautiful Scientist and Technologists."

HAN QIWEI

The Legendary Academician Who Grew up from "Narrow Streams" into "Great Rivers"

Han Qiwei's experience was legendary because he was an academician of the Chinese Academy of Engineering who never formally attended a university. From Han's point of view, his young age and low education level had never been an insurmountable obstacle to climb the high peak of science. He believed that with his efforts, a stream can grow into a great river and he can reach the height he looked up to. With his love and dedication to the cause of sediment, he has solved many difficult problems in sediment and achieved groundbreaking results.

HAN QIWEI (1933–2019), born in Songzi, Hongbei Province, was a member of the Communist Party of China. He was an expert on sediment and riverbed evolution, an academician of the Chinese Academy of Engineering, and a first-grade professor-level senior engineer of China Institute of Water Resources and Hydropower Research. In 1950, Han Qi became a staff member of the Shashi Hydrological Station of Yangtze River Conservancy Committee. From 1961 to 1965, he left his job and went to Wuhan Institute of Hydraulic and Electric Engineering (now Wuhan University)

Han Qiwei

and Department of Mathematics of Wuhan University for further study. From 1965 to 1980, he worked in Changjiang River Scientific Research Institute. In 1980, he was transferred to China Institute of Water Resources and Hydropower Research.

Han Qiwei had long been engaged in the research on sediment movement theory, reservoir sedimentation, riverbed evolution and engineering sediment. He established the statistical theory system of sediment movement and laid the foundation of sediment theory research. In 1984, he published *The Statistical Theory of Sediment Movement*, which was the crystallization of his research on sediment movement statistics and reservoir siltation and has been widely recognized by his peers at home and abroad. Han Qi established a relatively complete statistical theory system of sediment movement for methods that combine mechanics and stochastic process, which had a remarkable groundbreaking impact. It was evaluated as "international leading level," and played a role in advancing the development of sediment movement theory.

The study won the third price of the National Award for Natural Sciences in 1993. In reservoir siltation, he carried out special research on unbalanced sediment transport, density current, siltation pattern, fluctuating backwater area flushing, backwater elevation, dry density of siltation, and reservoir siltation control, etc. He completed the transition from qualitative description to quantitative expression of reservoir siltation. At the same time, he also conducted in-depth research on the riverbed deformation, sediment concentration recovery, riverbed sediment coarsening, and river pattern transformation. His research revealed the sediment incipient motion mechanism and studied its statistical law, the unification of sediment transport rate and incipient motion, the quantitative standard of incipient motion, the incipient motion of heterogeneous sediment groups, and the incipient motion of fine particle agglomeration.

Reservoir Siltation

Han Qiwei studied the unbalanced transport of heterogeneous suspended sediment in-depth and has achieved many breakthroughs and innovations in the bottom boundary conditions of diffusion equation, the gradation of sediment carrying capacity, saturation recovery coefficient, the exchange of coarse and fine sediment, the unified movement law of bed material, and flushing sediment, etc. It was the first formal mathematical model to calculate reservoir sedimentation in China. This model was later applied to the prediction of the Three Gorges Reservoir sedimentation, which provided a strong technical support for the project, and was widely used in the study of the sedimentation of many large and medium-sized reservoirs. In 1988, the research won the third prize of the State's Science and Technology Advancement Award.

The Statistical Theory of Bed Load Movement

The one-dimensional mathematical model theory of reservoir sedimentation and riverbed evolution established by Hanqi has strong theoretical basis, complete functions, detailed sediment calculation, fixed parameters and good universality, reaching international advanced level. He conducted many researches on sediment in reservoir projects at Danjiangkou, Gezhouba, Three Gorges, Datengxia, Dongfeng, Xiangjiaba, Sanmenxia, and Xiaolangdi. He had long been in charge of the study on the sedimentation of the Three Gorges Reservoir and the river channel evolution in the lower reaches, revealing the principle, technical feasibility, and economic rationality of the project. Han Qiwei also conducted in-depth research and held unique opinions on the lake relationship and flood transformation in the middle reaches of the Yangtze River, the riverbed evolution in the lower reaches of the Yellow River, and the radical cure of the Huai River.

Hanqi devoted his whole life to the study of sediment movement, created a number of innovative achievements in bed load diffusion and single sediment movement, opened up several fields such as bed-surface sediment exchange and stochastic model of sediment transport rate, laid the theoretical foundation of reservoir sedimentation, and made significant contributions to the cause of sediment control in China.

ZHANG CHUHAN

The Scholar Who "Rooted in the Ground and Aimed for the Sky"

Academician Zhang Chuhan once said, "'Root in the ground' means to base the research on the engineering practice of the country. 'Reach the sky' refers to aim at the scientific frontiers of the world, conduct systematic research persistently with long-term planning... 'Study hard, think hard and trace back to the roots' is the upper scroll of my motto, 'Discipline yourself to help others, pursue honesty and beauty,' is the lower scroll. We cultivate noble moral quality to 'Discipline ourselves to help others.' We need to stay kind and honest."

ZHANG CHUHAN, born in 1933 in Meizhou, Guangdong, was an expert in water conservancy and hydropower, an academician of Chinese Academy of Sciences, and a professor of Tsinghua University. He had stayed in Tsinghua as a teacher since he graduated from the Department of Water Resources of the university in 1957. He served as the head of Beijing Miyun Reservoir Aseismic Reinforcement Design Group from 1976 to 1978. He was a visiting scholar in the Department of Civil Engineering and Seismic Engineering Research Center of the University of California, Berkeley

Zhang Chuhan

from 1978 to 1981. Since 1983, he participated in the technical research projects of the seventh, eighth and nineth Five-Year Plan of China, focusing on the theory and method of aseismic safety analysis of high arch dams in combination with the national task of high dam construction. From 1988 to 2000, he was employed as a part-time adjunct professor at Concordia University in Montreal, Canada.

Zhang Chuhan conducted research closely combining the practice of China's hydraulic and hydropower high dam projects, carefully studied the high dam aseismic issues, achieved breakthrough in the applied basic theory, analysis model and evaluation system of the failure mechanism of dynamic and static force of high dam, filling in the blank of related fields. He proposed the analysis model of nonlinear dynamic damage cracking of high dam foundation reservoir water system, which could take the infinite radiation damping of the foundation, geometric nonlinearity of transverse joints, and other key factors into account. He proposed the simulation analysis model of the discontinuous whole process of dynamic and static force overload failure of high dam, completing the simulation of the whole process of continuous crack and discontinuous failure of high dam under dynamic and static load. He proposed an engineering analogy method to predict the safety status of newly-built high dams and a three grades bearing capacity evaluation index, which established a high dam safety evaluation system that is both scientific and practical for projects. He developed a meso-mechanical simulation model that simulates concrete aggregate, mortar and interface, which deepened the industry's understanding of the dynamic characteristics of concrete materials. All achievements above had been widely applied in high dam projects in China, which solved the key technical problems of high dam safety evaluation and advanced the development of high dam hydropower station construction in China.

In terms of engineering practice, Zhang Chuhan and his team completed the key technical research and safety evaluation of more than 30 high dams projects including Three Gorges, Ertan, Xiaowan, Xiluodu, and Jinping. During the consultation for major national hydraulic and hydropower projects, he presided over or participated in projects such as the South-North Water Diversion Project, the development of large-scale hydropower stations in the southwest, the protection and development of Nujiang River, the regulation of Tangjiashan barrier lake and the protection of Beichuan earthquake ruins, the development strategy of hydraulic discipline, the development of ecological water city in Xiong'an New Area, and the water and engineering strategy of the Yellow River, etc.

Zhang Chuhan applied dynamic boundary element method and fracture mechanics theory in his research. He proposed the propagation model of gravity dam seismic fracture and arch dam crack. He developed it into anisotropic medium and nonlinear concrete material with demonstration through dynamic crack experiment, which was applied in the aseismic design of several concrete earth dams. He put forward a coupled model of dynamic boundary element and discrete element model in time domain, which was applied in the stability forecast of large-scale underground powerhouse and high slope deformation of Three Gorges navigation lock.

Zhang Chuhan successively won more than 20 awards above provincial and ministerial level, including the third prize of National Natural Science Award, the second prize of the State's Science and Technology Advancement Award, the National Science and Technology Conference Award, the first prize of National Excellent Teaching Achievement, and the Outstanding Contribution Award and Ye Jianying Award of Tsinghua University. He was a member of the American Society of Civil Engineers, an honorary director of the Chinese Hydraulic Engineering Society, an executive director of the Chinese Society of Large Dam Engineering, a member of the Science and Technology Committee of the Ministry of Water Resources, a judge of the National Science and Technology Award, and an editor of *Journal of Earthquake and Tsunami*, *Earthquake Engineering and Engineering Vibration*, and other international publications.

SHEN ZHUJIANG

The Founder of "The Model of Nanjing Hydraulics"

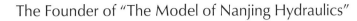

The research led by Shen Zhujiang was numerical analysis and research, which was highly theoretical, technological, pioneering with great workload, while its economic benefits were usually low. It was a "hard nut" with long research cycles and high difficulty. However, Shen Zhujiang always followed the needs of the country without haggling. He valued national interests regardless of his remuneration.

SHEN ZHUJIANG (1933–2006), born in Cixi, Zhejiang Province, was a geotechnical expert, academician of Chinese Academy of Sciences, senior engineer of Nanjing Hydraulic Research Institute, and professor of Department of Water Resources and Hydropower Engineering of Tsinghua University.

He graduated from East China Institute of Water Conservancy (now Hohai University) in 1953 and obtained the candidate of doctoral degree of Moscow State University of Civil Engineering in 1960. He was involved in research projects such as the deformation control of Shanghai Port terminal and the stability of Bohai Bay offshore drilling vessel. In his later work, he combined the static analysis theory of Soviet scholars with the motion analysis theory of American scholars, established the soil limit

Shen Zhujiang

analysis theory, and put forward the effective consolidation stress method of foundation stability analysis of soft soils. Since the 1970s, he had been engaged in the research on constitutive model and numerical calculation method of soil, put forward new concepts such as multiple yield surface, equivalent stress hardening theory, and triangle shear failure criterion, advised two new elasto-plastic models, developed effective stress analysis method, and created six finite element analysis programs, which was widely used in the calculation of large earth-rockfill dam engineering. He opened up a new direction for the research on soil structural model, proposed a new cemented rod element and a double-spring model based on damage, and assumed the fundamental framework of modern soil mechanics, which was the three basic theories of progressive soil failure, unsaturated soil consolidation, and liquefaction failure. It covered field including calculation, engineering, experiment, application, and made outstanding contributions to the theoretical development and academic innovation of soil mechanics and geotechnical engineering in China.

Shen Zhujiang devoted himself to studying soil mechanics, which was the basic discipline of civil engineering and hydraulics. He obtained abundant achievements in the calculation of soft foundation and earth-rockfill dam construction. Shen Zhujiang established the "The Model of Nanjing Hydraulics" (an "elastic-plastic constitutive model of soil" developed in late 1970s that was named by its birth places Nanjing Hydraulic Research Institute), a testimony to his successful academic research career. This model has been applied to develop the calculation program of the strain analysis of the earth-rockfill dam's total stress method, and contributed to the construction of the Three Gorges deep-water cofferdam and the Tianshengqiao Hydropower Station. The other research focus of Shen Zhujiang was unsaturated soil. The main canal project at the middle line of China's major project South-North Water Diversion, which extended from Danjiangkou to Beijing, was in unsaturated soil. The research on this area was related to the safety of the project. Shen Zhujiang led the team to research unsaturated soil and completed the theoretical preparation for the national scientific and technological research project "Slope Stability of the Main Canal Project of South-North Water Diversion," of the Nineth Five-year Plan of China.

Shen Zhujiang participated in the research and consultation on the key technical issues of many major projects in China including the Three Gorges deep-water cofferdam, Xiaolangdi Dam of the Yellow River, Port of Tianjin and Shanghai Port, which made important contributions to the hydraulic, hydropower and water transportation undertakings in China. In 1994, Shen Zhu-jiang was elected as the chief editor of *Geotechnical Engineering Journal*. Under his leadership, the journal became an important publication popular in China's geotechnical engineering field.

As a well-known scholar and deputy to the National People's Congress, Shen Zhujiang not only worked hard and conscientiously in his profession to overcome more scientific challenges, but also paid close attention to the development of the country and its society, actively advising on environmental issues with constant efforts. With his enthusiasm for scientific research and deep love for the motherland, he reviewed papers and manuscripts tirelessly in his study and earnestly taught and cared for students at school. All these efforts reflected his scientific spirit with diligence, rigor, pragmatism, innovation, and his strong sense of responsibility to the country and society.

Geotechnical Engineering Journal

LUO SHAOJI

A Wave Rider in Guangdong Province

Luo Shaoji said, "If I had some achievements in hydropower projects, it also accredited to China's economic development. Due to the reform and opening, we achieved better economic development." As a pioneer and developer in pumped storage technology, he recognized that the progress of science and technology and the improvement of people's living conditions closely relied on great national strategies. He rooted himself in the broad platform given by the state and served the urgent needs of the state and its people. He always insisted on reform thinking, open vision and guided his thoughts and actions with the motto "be bold enough to innovate and practice."

LUO SHAOJI, born in Nanhai, Guangdong Province in 1933, was a member of the Communist Party of China, an expert in power generation engineering and an academician of the Chinese Academy of Engineering.

In 1951, Luo Shaoji was admitted to the water resources utilization major of Department of Water Resources of Tsinghua University. After graduation in 1955, he started working in the Central South Investigation and Design Institute of the Ministry of Electric Power Industry. He successively held the

Luo Shaoji

positions of technician, engineer, chief design engineer, senior engineer, vice president, and president. In 1985, he served as the director of China Southern Power Grid Office of the Ministry of Water Resources and Electric Power. Since 1988, he successively served as the deputy director of Guangdong Electric Power Industry Bureau and the general manager and professor-level senior engineer of Guangdong Pumped Storage Power Station Joint Venture. In 1995, he was awarded the "National Model Worker." In 1999, he was elected as academician of the Chinese Academy of Engineering. From 1997 to 2005, he served as consultant and professor-level senior engineer of Guangdong Pumped Storage Power Generation Co., Ltd., member of Guangdong Provincial Science and Technology Association, honorary director of China Society for Hydroelectric Engineering, honorary director of Guangdong Society for Hydroelectric Engineering, deputy head of expert group for construction quality inspection of Three Gorges Project, and consulting expert of several domestic pumped storage power stations.

In the 1970s, he worked as the chief engineer of Fengtan Hydropower Station in Hunan Province and successfully organized and designed China's first powerhouse inside hollow gravity arch dam with a height of 112.5 m, which solved the contradiction between the layout of narrow river valley powerhouse layout and large flood discharge and saved project cost.

At the end of the 1980s, he switched his work from hydropower design to hydropower station construction and management, created an innovative path in the practice of hydropower station construction, and made outstanding contributions to hydropower construction in China. In 1988, Luo

Shaoji was transferred to the position of Deputy Director of Guangdong Electric Power Bureau and General Manager of Guangdong Pumped Storage Power Station Joint Venture, where he was responsible for organizing the construction of Guangzhou Pumped Storage Power Station, the first high-head and large-capacity pumped storage power station in China with the largest installed capacity in the world at that time. Although the construction schedule was tight with difficult site conditions, he worked side by side with the workers and ate and lived together with them in the pool. Under his leadership, project builders overcame various difficulties and solved key technical problems by introducing technology and cooperation. The project construction's scientific research achievements "Research and Practice of Key Technologies for Construction of Guangzhou Pumped Storage Power Station" won the second prize of the State's Science and Technology Advancement Award in 1997 and the first prize of Guangdong Province Science and Technology Advancement Award in 1995. The survey and design of Phase I of Guangzhou Pumped Storage Power Station won the silver and gold awards of National Excellent Investigation and Design respectively. The investigation and design of the Phase II of the Project won the silver and bronze awards of National Excellent Survey and Design respectively. The construction of Guangzhou Pumped Storage Power Station achieved the goal of kicking off the construction of China Pumped Storage Power Station at a high level even with its late start. The project's comprehensive technology reached the world advanced level and its successful experience has been gradually promoted in the national hydropower station management, which greatly improved the management level of China hydropower stations.

Luo Shaoji carried out a highly effective reform in the construction of Guangzhou Pumped Storage Power Station. It included the reform of construction management system to implement project legal person responsibility system and the reform of operation system to establish a set of unattended and less-attended management model, which enabled China to become one of the few countries with unattended million-kilowatt hydropower plants. The management reform of the project was the first practice of leasing capacity operation and broadened the development of China's pumped storage power station.

After his retirement, Luo Shaoji also served as a consultant of Shandong Tai'an Pumped Storage Power Station, a member the expert group of Yunnan Dachaoshan Hydropower Station, and a member of the World Bank's Special Advisory Group for Anhui Tongbai Pumped Storage Power Station, contributing his efforts to China's hydropower industry.

LU YOUMEI

Who Went through Difficulties to Develop the Three Gorges

"Should I stay in my hometown Shanghai and enjoy the prosperous city life, or leave for exploring the world? Lu Youmei wondered. "A great man has the ambition of conquering the world!" Thought of that, Lu Youmei went to the site of Liujiaxia Hydropower Station on the Yellow River and stayed for 14 years.

LU YOUMEI, a native of Taicang, Jiangsu Province, was born in Shanghai in 1934. He was a member of the Chinese Communist Party, an expert in hydraulic and hydropower engineering, an academician of the Chinese Academy of Engineering and a professor and a doctoral supervisor of Hohai University.

In 1956, Lu Youmei graduated from East China Institute of Water Conservancy (now Hohai University) with a major in river structure and hydropower generation. From 1956 to 1970, he participated in the construction of Liujiaxia Hydropower Station on the Yellow River, serving as the head of the technical section of Liujiaxia Hydropower

Lu Youmei

Engineering Bureau. From 1970 to 1975, he participated in the construction of Shiquan Hydropower Station on the Han River, serving as the head of the technical section of the Engineering Bureau 15 of the Ministry of Water Resources and Electric Power. From 1975 to 1983, he joined and organized the construction of Ankang Hydropower Station on the Han River as the director, chief engineer, and deputy Director of the Engineering Bureau 3 of the Ministry of Water Resources and Electric Power. From 1983 to 1984, he organized the construction of Longyangxia Hydropower Station on the Yellow River as the director of the Engineering Bureau 4 of the Ministry of Water Resources and Electric Power. From 1984 to 1988, he served as Vice Minister of Water Resources and Electric Power. From 1988 to 1992, he was the Vice Minister of Energy. From 1993 to 2003, he worked as the General Manager of China Three Gorges Corporation; In 2003, he was elected as an academician of the Chinese Academy of Engineering.

After graduating from East China Institute of Water Conservancy, Lu Youmei left the bustling city behind, packed his luggage, and went to Liujiaxia Hydropower Station site on the Yellow River full of enthusiasm. He started to refine himself in the vast northwest region of China. From Liujiaxia Dam to Shiquan Reservoir, Ankang dam, and Longyangxia Dam, Lu Youmei accumulated enormous knowledge and experience in engineering practice, followed by another and improved his expertise and organization and leadership ability.

Upon receiving the position transfer order, Lu Youmei came to Beijing to serve as the Vice Minister of Water Resources and Electric Power. In eight years, he promoted the reform of the hydropower construction

The Three Gorges Project

system, participated in the demonstration of the Three Gorges Project, and served as the vice chairman of the demonstration leading group. He cooperated with many experts with rigorous scientific attitude and completed the final demonstration report of the Three Gorges Project. He completed a lot of work to facilitate the launch of the Three Gorges Project. He advanced the formation of the China southern power grid and achieved the early-stage West-to-east Power Transmission. In 1993, as a member of the Three Gorges Project Construction Committee of the State Council and the General Manager of China Three Gorges Corporation, Lu Youmei led the construction of the Three Gorges Project. He successfully explored and carried out the "Three Gorges Model." The project was a great mission with a duration of 17 years, which covered the construction of this magnificent project and the rolling development of water conservancy and hydropower in the upper reaches of the Yangtze River. Lu Youmei was bold enough to take on the heavy burden and faced the difficulties confidently. Lu Youmei grew from an ordinary engineer to the director of construction, the Vice Minister of Hydropower, and the general manager of China Three Gorges Corporation, commanding thousands of workers. The hard practice he completed through the cause of hydropower construction trained him into a leader style expert specializing both in hydropower and management.

In 2002, he received the Lifetime Achievement Award from the International Commission on Large Dams. In 2015 he received the Engineering Achievement Award of World Federation of Engineering Organizations.

LIU CHANGMING

Whose Heart Was Full of Love for Rivers

When Liu Changming was studying in Moscow State University, he was asked by his teacher why he chose hydrology and water resources as his major. He answered, "First, water resources are closely related to human production and life; Second, China is one of the countries that lack water resources, so I chose hydrology and water resources to satisfy my country's demand." He strongly agreed with Einstein's theory of relativity and believed that there are only relativities in the universe, no absolutes. He said, "Just like the theory of relativity, even if a person has achieved certain success, he still needs to learn and study. Knowledge is limited, but not learning. There is no end for learning."

LIU CHANGMING, born in Miluo, Hunan Province in 1934, was an expert in hydrology and water resources. He was an academician of the Chinese Academy of Sciences and a researcher and doctoral supervisor of the Institute of Geology and Resources of the Chinese Academy of Sciences.

In 1956, Liu Changming graduated from Northwestern University with honors and was assigned to work at the Institute of Geography of the Chinese Academy of Sciences. In 1960, he went to study in the Department of Geography of Moscow University.

Liu Changming

After he returned to China from his studies, Liu Changming founded the first laboratory of artificial rainfall runoff in China at the Institute of Geography of the Chinese Academy of Sciences. In the late 1960s, he derived and composed the formula for calculating the maximum flow rate of small watersheds and studied the spatio-temporal distribution of storm water, the overland flow concentration of infiltration runoff, etc. In 1978, the method for calculating small watersheds' peak flood flow rate won the National Science and Technology Conference Award.

Liu Changming developed the research of hydrology and water resources with focus in geology and made many achievements in water circulation, flow runoff, concentration patterns, hydrological experiments, agricultural hydrology, forest hydrology, ecological and environmental hydrology, and the impact of climate change and human activities on hydrology and water resources. He combined the earth physics and engineering concentrations in hydrology with disciplines like farmland water conservancy, realized innovations in hydrology and water resources research and solved the difficulty of storm water calculation of small watersheds of regions that lack data. In the study of the environmental impact of the South-North Water Diversion, he developed systematic geographic system analysis and established models. The multi-water conversion theory he proposed during the study of hydrological processes, water conversion, and regulation deepened the water circulation theory. It advocated the transformation of rainwater into water resources, which was conceptually innovative.

In response to the national planning of the South-North Water Diversion Project, he proposed the method of hydrographic system analysis of water transfer, developed the application of regional water division and heat theory methods in water allocation, and put forward the evaluation method of the project's impact on the environment. Regarding the problem of agricultural water supply for grain production, he proposed the systematic theory of water-saving agriculture, undertook the research of Yellow Sea and Huaihai during the Seventh Five-Year Plan period, organized and led many projects of the Eighth Five-Year Plan such as the "National Major Fund" and "Applied Basic Research on Major Water-saving Agriculture in North China." He also developed and enriched the theory of water-saving agriculture with new perspectives including the transformation of "five waters,"[1] the "four balances" theory of regional water resources development and ecological protection, the evaluation method of agricultural water resources and the interfacial theory and division of the movement control of farmland water, providing consultation and research for national water resources issues. From 1999 to 2004, he completed the major project "Evolution Law and the Renewability Maintenance Mechanism of the Water Resources of Yellow River" of the "973 Plan"[2] of China.

He was the groundbreaker of genetic hydrology, a pioneer of hydrological prediction in China's ungauged areas, the founder of the first artificial rainfall runoff laboratory in China, and the proponent of the water science connotation that combines "resource-ecological environment-disaster engineering." He was committed to "interpreting" and "understanding" water, "reducing the outflow" and "broadening the sources" of water resources and proposed the concept and evaluation method of "healthy river." Liu Changming was a guardian of water resources.

---

1. TN: Five water stands for wastewater regulation, flood control, flood drainage, water supplies protection, and water-saving execution.

2. TN: 973 Plan is China's development plan for its major basic researches.

WANG SIJING

A Geotechnical Expert Who Was Good at Thinking and Took Studying Seriously

In 1954, Sijing Wang, who was only 20 years old, departed from Manzhouli with his classmates to study at Moscow Geological Prospecting Institute, where he began his eight-year-long overseas study. "When the train passed through the Ural Mountains, we saw many modern factories through the windows," Wang Sijing said, "At that moment, I was keenly aware of the gap between our countries and Russia. It was also that moment when decided to learn the most advanced technology and come back to develop our motherland."

WANG SIJING, whose family was from Anhui Province, was born in Shanghai in 1934. He was an expert in engineering geology, environmental geology, rock mechanics, and the Chinese Academy of Engineering academician. He graduated from the Moscow Geological Prospecting Institute of the Soviet Union in 1959 with the title of geological engineer and as a doctoral degree candidate from the Institute of Geology and Mineralogy of the USSR Academy in 1963.

Wang Sijing had long been devoted to the research combining geology with mechanics and engineering and made

Wang Sijing

significant contributions to rock mass structure theory and engineering geomechanics. He developed the principles and methods of stability analysis of rock mass engineering based on the research of deformation and facture mechanism of rock mass engineering. He proposed the theory of dependence and interaction between human engineering activities and geological environment. He led the research on the mutual influence and constraints of engineering construction and geological environment, which opened up the field of environmental engineering geology and provided the theoretical basis for the research on geological environment of engineering and urban development.

Wang Sijing studied and demonstrated several major water conservancy and hydropower projects, providing the basis for solving key geological problems. He participated in and directed the geological and seismic demonstration during the early stage of Three Gorges Project and conducted a comprehensive multidisciplinary demonstration of the feasibility and engineering geological conditions of the Yalong River Ertan Hydropower Station including remote sensing, geology, and rock mechanics. He undertook the research, consultation, and evaluation of Xiaolangdi Dam on the Yellow River, Longtan Dam on the Hongshui River, Xiangjiaba Dam on the Jinsha River, Tiger Leaping Gorge, and Guangzhou Pumped Storage Power Station. He evaluated the stability of shotcrete-bolt support and caverns for several un-

The Longtan Dam on the Hongshui River

derground large national defense projects on the third line. He made many contributions to geological research on Jinchuan Nickel Mine, underground nuclear explosions, and its engineering protection.

Wang Sijing successively carried out research on environmental geology and urban development planning in the Xichang area of Panzhihua and established the earliest urban geological information system of Panzhihua. He conducted research on geological environment in Beijing and other cities, and participated in the research on landslide hazards and information system in Hong Kong, which made important progress.

He had been employed by several universities and was an honorary professor at the University of Hong Kong and Tongji University, a visiting professor at the University of Western Ontario (now Westhampton University) in Canada, the University of Catania in Italy, as well as Nanjing University, Sun Yat-sen University, and Jilin University. He served as the director of the academic committee of the National Frozen-ground Engineering Laboratory and Engineering Geomechanics Laboratory of the Chinese Academy of Sciences. His work included *Engineering Geomechanics Analysis of Dam Foundation Stability*, *Geotechnical Stability Analysis of Underground Construction*, *Geoenvironmental Consideration in the Strategic Planning of Regional Development*, and other monographs.

Wang Sijing received many awards, including the First Prize of Scientific and Technological Achievement Award of Chinese Academy of Sciences and the Third Prize of National Natural Science Award, He also won Hans Cloos Award, the highest academic award of International Association of Engineering Geology and Environment (IAEG). He was also awarded the Outstanding Contribution Award of Southeast Asian Geotechnical Society. He was elected as the president of the International Association of Geoscientists for Development (AGID) in 1987, president of the Chinese Society for Rock Mechanics and Engineering in 1998, and president of the International Association of Engineering Geology and Environment (IAEG) in the same year. Wang Sijing enjoyed a high reputation in the international geotechnical community.

GE XIURUN

Whose Career in Rock Mass Engineering Was as Firm as a Monolith

After returning from the Soviet Union, Ge Xiurun did not choose to work in Shanghai, but went to the Wuhan Institute of Rock and Soil Mechanics following the country's demand. He said, "I am a Shanghai native, it was certainly good to work in Shanghai, with my family and friends around. But the country needed me to work in Wuhan, where I could give full play to my professional strengths. The young people from our era were simple-minded, we thought very little about ourselves, but we valued the interests and needs of our country above everything else. I think we should always put the country's interests first and not care too much about personal gains and losses. Suppose the experts who researched and developed atomic bombs, rockets and satellites only thought about their interests without any spirit of patriotism and dedication. How could they achieve world-renowned achievements?"

GE XIURUN, born in Shanghai in 1934, was a member of the Chinese Communist Party, an expert in geotechnics, an academician of the Chinese Academy of Engineering, a researcher at the Wuhan Institute of Rock and Soil Mechanics of the Chinese Academy of Sciences, director of the Academic Committee of the Key Laboratory of Rock and Soil Mechanics of the Chinese Academy of Sciences, and director of the Institute of Geotechnical Engineering of Shanghai Jiaotong University.

Ge Xiurun

After studying at Tsinghua University for one year, Ge Xiurun went to the Soviet Union to study at the Department of Hydraulic Engineering of the Odessa State Academy of Civil Engineering and Architecture. He graduated with as a candidate of doctoral degree in 1959. After returning to China in the same year, he started working as a researcher at the Wuhan Institute of Geotechnics of Chinese Academy of Sciences and director of its Geotechnical Research Department.

Ge Xiurun had been engaged in the scientific research of rock and soil mechanics and major geotechnical projects for a long time and was one of the discipline leaders in the field of rock slope research in China. The research on the south slope of Daye Iron Mine, which started in the early 1960s, was a famous project that first combined large-scale in-situ test in China. It broke a new ground and a new stage for the slope research in China. Xiu Run overcame the difficulties and completed the stability analysis calculation report and rock mechanics test summary of the slope research task. He successively presided over and participated in researching more than ten major engineering projects of rock foundation of dams, underground caverns, and especially rock slopes. He presided over large-scale mine slope projects such as Tonglingshan Copper Mine, Yongping Copper Mine, Hainan Iron Mine, and the dam stability evaluation and remediation projects of special earth dams such as Yinshan Lead-Zinc Mine and Wushan Copper Mine Tailings Dam, which created significant social and economic benefits. He presided over the completion of north slope landslide remediation and monitoring work of Daye Iron Mine, which was evaluated by the appraisal committee as "international advanced level and a model for slope projects of same category," and won the first prize of Hubei Provincial Science and Technology Advancement Award in 1994. His work "Research on the Expansion and Mechanical Properties of Eroded Granite in Guangzhou Pumped Storage Power Station" won the second prize in Science and Technology Advancement Award of Chinese Academy of Sciences in 1990.

Ge Xiurun was regarded as "one of the earliest pioneers who introduced finite element method into China's rock engineering research." The finite element program that was capable of solving large plane problems led and written by him for the domestic X1 machine had been widely used. In 1974, he presided over the completion of the nonlinear finite element analysis of the stability of the Gezhouba dam's Erjiang floodgate, which won the State Science and Technology Advancement Award in 1985, contributing to the construction

The Erjiang Floodgate of Gezhouba Dam

of the Gezhouba dam project. In 1978, he led the research on "Rock Mechanics Application and Nonlinear Analysis Method of Finite Element Method," which was awarded the Major Scientific Research Accomplishment Award by the Chinese Academy of Sciences. The achievement of the research "Finite Element Analysis of Deep Anti-slipping Stability of Section 1#-5# of the Left Plant of the Three Gorges Project," which he presided over, played a very important role in settling the argument over the most major rock mechanics issue in the Three Gorges Project for more than ten years and was adopted in the technical design of the Three Gorges Dam. His work on "Finite Element Nonlinear Analysis of the Gravity Arch Dam of the Geheyan Hydropower Station" won the third prize in the State Science and Technology Advancement Award in 1990. His collaborative work on "Three-dimensional Infinite Elements and Joint Infinite Elements" won the third prize in the Natural Science Award of the Chinese Academy of Sciences in 1990.

As a geotechnical engineering expert, Ge Xiurun had made a large number of important research results for the large-scale hydropower engineering field in China and has made significant contributions to China's water conservancy and hydropower undertakings.

XIE SHILENG

Who Spent His Life along the Coast

In light of Xie Shileng's status as an "advanced student" and the actual level of port and coastal engineering in China at that time, Prof. Baikel assigned Xie Shileng to conduct the internal force analysis of waves on the artificial armor blocks of seawalls. When Xie Shileng heard this, his heart sank, "I could conduct this type of research in China too. If I cannot learn the core technology of Prof. Baikel, how can I improve the development level of domestic ports and serve my country?" He boldly expressed his thoughts, which surprised Professor Baikel but also moved him by Xie Shileng's patriotic enthusiasm and thirst for knowledge. He let Xie Shileng study wave scouring theory, the most cutting-edge at that time, which later became his specialty.

XIE SHILENG (1935–2018), whose family was from Cixi, Ningbo, was born in Shanghai. He was a member of the Communist Party of China, an expert in port and coastal engineering design, a Chinese engineering design master, and an academician of the Chinese Academy of Engineering.

He graduated from Dalian Institute of Technology (now Dalian University of Technology) in 1956. He served as a technician of the Water Transport Design Institute of the Ministry of Transportation and Communications, director of the design office, deputy chief engineer, and senior technical advisor of the First Design Institute of Naval Engineering of the Ministry of Transportation and Communications. After 1985, he was also involved in the new extension projects of the caisson terminals of Berths 8 and 9 and the breakwater of Port of Qinhuangdao as well as the design of the breakwater project of Port of Qingdao and the Dagu Lighthouse of Port of Tianjin.

Xie Shileng

In 1979, Xie Shileng studied at Delft University of Technology in the Netherlands as a visiting scholar. In 1981, he proposed a method for calculating the seafloor scour in front of upright breakwaters. After the paper's publication, its results were cited in the literature of many countries. The method was also called "Xie's theory" and "Xie's formula," which was incorporated into the breakwater standard of the Ministry of Transportation at that time and included in the *Coastal Engineering Manual* of the United States. After returning to China in the same year, Xie Shileng concluded a number of research results combining the characteristics of Chinese ports and coasts. His work was unique in hydraulic structures, particularly in deep-water breakwaters. He had deep knowledge and abundant achievement in harbour hydrology and made significant contribution to Chinese port design and coastal engineering.

From 1998 to 1999, Shileng Xie proposed a calculation formula of wave on a semicircular breakwater under inundation, which was adopted in the deep-water channel regulation project at the estuary of the Yangtze River.

Xie Shileng has completed over 100 design and research projects, among which more than 40 were national key and medium to large-sized projects. He has successively won the gold and silver award of National Design Excellence Award and six silver awards of National Quality Award. He also won the first prize of the State's Science and Technology Advancement Award once, the second and third prize for three times. He won the Innovative Technology Star Award of United Nations, with three of his research projects awarded National Patent Grant. In 1999, he was awarded the "Chinese Engineering Design Master" title and elected as an academician of the Chinese Academy of Engineering.

LI PEICHENG

A Persistent Water Seeker in Northwest China

"Our generation abides by the academic tradition inherently, which means we always insist on seeking facts, truth, and pragmatism in the practice of scientific research. To seek facts is to respect the law and pursue the truth; to seek the truth is to seek truth from facts and to be scientifically rigorous; pragmatism is to be beneficial to the world and the future, to serve the country and the people." This was Li Peicheng's way of learning and his lifelong academic belief.

LI PEICHENG, born in 1934 in Qian County, Shaanxi Province, was a member of the Chinese Communist Party, an expert in agricultural soil and water engineering and water resources and environment. He was also an academician of the Chinese Academy of Engineering and a professor and doctoral supervisor of Chang'an University.

After graduating from high school in 1952, Li Peicheng enrolled in the Department of Water Resources of the Northwest Agricultural College, where he graduated with full honors in 1956 and stayed as a teacher. In 1958, He passed the screening test for graduate studies in Soviet Union and eventually departed after several setbacks. He completed the thesis as a candidate of doctoral degree early and systematically proposed the theory of "cut-off well method" for seepage calculation, derived the corre-

Li Peicheng

sponding calculation formula, and digitally plotted the supporting calculation diagrams. After returning to China, he taught at Xi'an Jiaotong University and Shaanxi University of Technology.

Li Peicheng presided over the construction of the Fuping underground reservoir test project, took charge in the survey and design of the re-routing project of the main canal of Jinghui Canal, and led the completion and installation of the first large hydraulic integrator in China. He completed a lot of foundational work to establish an engineering and technology system for groundwater development and utilization in agriculture.

He created the "cut-off well method" theory for calculating the seepage of drainage and irrigation well clusters, which helped solve major problems in well cluster design. He successfully developed the yellow soil radiation well through collaboration, of which the water output was 8–12 times higher than other local wall types. His achievement was promoted to more than 10 cities and has theoretically broken the traditional idea that loess cannot become aquifer, winning the National Science Conference Award. His research on light wells won the fourth prize of the National Invention Award. He also proposed the forward-looking theory of "unified observation and management of three water[1]" and the corresponding

---

1. TN: "Three water" refers to surface water, groundwater, and rainwater.

technical methods used to prevent and control salinization and expand irrigation water sources. He was groundbreaking in furthering the development of agriculture and ecological environment in arid areas. He initiated and led the establishment of China's first research center for agriculture in arid areas and the International Research Center for Water Resources and Environment in Arid Areas.

In 1993, a large-scale water shortage broke out in Xi'an. Li Peicheng urgently submitted the proposal, *Connect Mountain to Form wells, Utilize Both Rivers and Mountain Waters: A Proposal on the Complete Solution to the Water Shortage Problem in Xi'an* to the relevant leaders of Shaanxi Province, in which he proposed the famous idea of "connect mountain to form wells, utilize both rivers and mountain waters to solve the water shortage in Xi'an," and successfully ended the water shortage in the city.

Since 2003, Li Peicheng has led six projects related to the "Science and Technology Action Plan for the Beauty of Northwest China's Mountains," which included the development of pilot demonstration areas of the beautiful mountains and research on major scientific and technological problems in different ecological regions of Northwest China, the study on the bearing capacity and sustainable utilization of groundwater resources in the oasis of the Alashan League Yaoba, and the construction of an innovation and intellectual introduction base of water security discipline and the hydrological ecology in arid and semi-arid areas, which provided technical support for recreating the beautiful Northwest China.

The main canal of Jinghui Canal

ZHANG YONGCHUAN

Whose Heart and Spirit Were as Clear and Inclusive as Water

During the War of Resistance, as a child, Zhang Yongchuan witnessed the tragic scenes where Japanese invaders ravaged his hometown and people fled everywhere, which inspired his goal of working hard for the country's prosperity. At the age of 18, he crossed the Bai River of his hometown by riding a little wooden boat. In 1954, when a once-in-a-century flood hit the Yangtze River, Zhang Yongchuan, a sophomore in college, was not afraid of the danger and went to the front line with his classmates for flood rescue. He always kept his family and motherland in mind and devoted himself to his career. He said, "How can we stay in the spring of our life forever? It demands us to put our youth, wisdom and strength into our career."

ZHANG YONGCHUAN, born in 1935, was a native of Nanyang, Henan Province. He was a member of the Communist Party of China, an expert in hydroelectric energy, a pioneer of hydropower in China, and an academician of the Chinese Academy of Engineering. He was also a professor and doctoral supervisor at Huazhong University of Science and Technology.

Zhong Yongchuan

In 1957, Zhang Yongchuan graduated from Huazhong University of Science and Technology with hydropower major and stayed on as a teacher. At the age of 28, he already compiled and published the book *Reservoir Scheduling of Hydropower Station*, which was the first book in the field of reservoir scheduling in China, showing his excellent scientific research ability and inquisitive spirit at that time.

In 1979, Zhang Yongchuan presided over the optimal scheduling of Zhexi Hydropower Station, which solved the difficult problems of inefficient and unbalanced power generation for this hydropower station that "feeds on the rainwater," making Zhexi Hydropower Station the first large and medium-sized power station in China to successfully achieve optimal scheduling. Subsequently, this achievement was promoted nationwide and applied to 34 hydropower stations across the country, creating huge economic benefits.

Zhang Yongchuan made important innovations in the basic theory, planning and decision making, risk management, and real-time control of reservoir operation, and has achieved several "first" in its respective category. He proposed the concept of "bias loss" for the first time, on the basis of which he created the calculation method of bias characteristic and the micro-increment principle for dealing with inter-reservoir compensation based on the characteristic and put forward the T-transform Kalman filter algorithm for multi-station runoff. He first proposed the discriminative principle of correlation link between multiple time periods, the essentials of direct correlation and transfer correlation, and derived the quantitative relationship between them. He provided the theoretical formula for describing the bias coefficient in runoff distribution by Markov chain. He established the concept of typical runoff process and the orthogonal efficient algorithm for typical decomposition of runoff. He initiated convex dynamic planning and water diversion game theory. He also proposed the concept of transfer correlation and its corresponding

Zhexi Hydropower Station

discriminant criterion and RBSI technology, which solved the "dimensional disaster" problem of reservoir optimization. He first developed the implicit stochastic decision-making model, flood classification, and classified inductive deductive forecasting model, which opened up a new approach for related studies. He first put forward the concept of "digital watershed" and carried out systematic research. He applied game theory, cybernetics, and uncertainty principle to hydropower and reservoir scheduling for the first time. His theories were applied to mega reservoirs and hydropower plants such as Danjiangkou Dam and Three Gorges Project.

Zhang Yongchuan made important contributions to the establishment and development of modern hydropower energy theory and modern reservoir operation theory by integrating hydroelectric energy theory, optimization theory, cybernetics theory, uncertainty principle, and technologies such as artificial intelligence, neural networks, and fuzzy analysis. His research results won the first and third prizes of the State Science and Technology Advancement Award.

While Zhang Yongchuan had been progressing on the road of innovation in scientific research, he was also fruitful in teaching in higher education with students all over the world. He had been working in Huazhong University of Science and Technology for half a century and trained many outstanding talents. In his old age, he served as the first president of Wenhua College of Huazhong University of Science and Technology, becoming the first academician to formally serve as the president of an independent college. There, he led his team to create the "Wenhua Miracle" in the history of the development of independent colleges.

CUI ZHENGQUAN

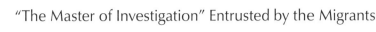

"The Master of Investigation" Entrusted by the Migrants

Cui Zhengquan lived a simple life, working for minimum payback and living with little demand, disciplining himself with the strict standard as a Communist Party member. Every time he visited the reservoir area, he had to remind the reception staff, "the country is still not rich enough, few vegetable dishes for my meal is enough, nothing lavish. It'd be a pity to waste them." When surveying the terrain, he always brought instant noodles and mineral water with him. Sometimes he just bought a few sweet potatoes from the villagers and used water to mix a bowl of cereal batter as a meal.

CUI ZHENGQUAN (1935–2005), born in Heilong County, Jilin Province, was a member of the Chinese Communist Party. He was a master of engineering investigation in China, a member of the Science and Technology Committee of the Ministry of Water Resources, a consultant of the Science and Technology Committee of the Yangtze River Conservancy Commission, and a chief engineer of the Comprehensive Survey Bureau of the Yangtze River Conservancy Commission.

Cui Zhengquan (in the middle) at work

In 1956, Cui Zhengquan graduated from the Department of Hydrology and Engineering Geology of Northeast Institute of Geology (now Changchun University of Science and Technology) with the ambition to devote himself to the cause of hydraulic geology of his motherland. After graduating from university, he worked in the Three Gorges brigade of the Ministry of Geology and was later assigned to the survey department of the Yangtze River Conservancy Commission, where he was responsible for geological surveys of hydropower stations on the Yangtze River. Cui Zhengquan gradually grown from the experience he accumulated through outdoor work and become a master in practice and pioneer in new technologies. In 1984, he returned from his overseas studies and became the deputy chief engineer of the survey head unit.

In 1991, Cui was appointed to be the general manager of the site selection and geological demonstration for the relocation of the Three Gorges Reservoir. This project had direct impact on the well-being of more than one million migrants in the reservoir area and the smooth implementation of the Three Gorges Project. The geological structure of the Three Gorges reservoir area was complex. Cui Zhengquan inspected the reservoir area many times a year, traveling thousands of kilometers and leaving his footprint over every corner of the Three Gorges reservoir area.

Through large amounts of detailed geological surveys and investigations, he finally figured out the geological condition of selected migration sites, providing geological basis for the site selection of urban migration and guiding the relocation work effectively. He was known as the "walking map" of the geology of Three Gorges reservoir area and the first person to prevent geological disasters in the reservoir area. After five years of painstaking efforts, Cui Zhengquan completed the selection of new sites for the relocation of the Three Gorges reservoir area with a high sense of responsibility and mission, providing preliminary and detailed geological survey reports of more than 10 million words and more than 10 thousands drawings, which saved losses of more than two billion yuan for developing new towns in the Three Gorges reservoir area in terms of site selection.

The full view of Wushan

He made great contributions to the Three Gorges Migration Project by doing his best to find a secure home for millions of migrants.

After migrants' new home was built, he proposed to establish a geological workstation in the reservoir area to monitor the geological disaster forecast and the operation of the new town in the long term, which became the guardian angel of the reservoir area and migrants' new home.

Cui Zhengquan also obtained great achievement in the aspect of scientific innovation. From 1984 to 1991, he was the deputy director of scientific research at his institute. He joined and presided over relevant national key projects, such as "Research on Systematic Engineering Geology and Geotechnical Engineering," which first created the theory of equilibrium between rock hydraulics and karst action. He established the theory and methodology of prediction of slope deformation and instability forecasting. He formulated the "Monitoring and Forecasting System of Slope Deformation and Instability of Yangtze River Three Gorges Project," which broke the ground in preventing and controlling geological disasters in the reservoir area. He introduced the concept of "dropped deposit" and guided the site selection of the new county town of Wushan based on it.

In addition to his busy job, Cui Zhengang wrote *Introduction to Systematic Engineering Geology*, which marked the establishment of his theory and methodology of "systematic engineering geology." The book won the Excellent Monograph Award of the Ministry of Water Resources, opened up a new field of engineering geology, and established the fifth school of international engineering geology.

In 1994, he was awarded the "Master of Engineering Survey in China." In 2007, the Ministry of Water Resources posthumously awarded him the honorary title of "Outstanding Expert in Hydraulic Technology."

CHEN DEJI

Whose Career Was Rooted in Rocks

Chen Deji endured the arduous journey of fieldwork and overcame all types of difficulties for decades. But he thought the most about the project and the stability of the dam foundation. He wanted to find a "home" for the dam but rarely thought about where to settle his own "cozy nest," never paying attention to personal gains and losses.

CHEN DEJI, born in 1935, was a native of Pingba, Guizhou Province, and a member of the Communist Party. He was one of the first batches of engineering geologists trained after the founding of the People's Republic of China and one of the first few masters of engineering survey in China.

Chen Deji graduated from the Water Resources Department of Liuzhou Senior School of Technology in 1953 and spent two years in 1957 in the Department of Hydrology and Engineering Geology of Beijing Institute of Geology (now China University of Geosciences) for further study. He had long been devoted to the geological investigation of hydraulic and hydropower projects. He was the chief engineer of the Head Survey Team of the Yangtze River Basin Planning Office, the director of the Comprehensive Survey Bureau of the Yangtze River Conservancy Commission, and the director of the Yangtze River Institute of Survey Technology. He was a witness to the development of the geological cause of the Yangtze River Conservancy Commission.

Chen Deji

After starting his career, Chen Deji and his colleagues carried out a series of special studies regarding the regional faults of the Danjiangkou Project and the geological structure of the dam area based on geomechanics theories. These research works not only helped clarify the controversies about the structural stability of the Danjiangkou Project at that time but also laid the foundation for the establishment of the Yangtze River Institute of Survey Technology later. During his career in hydrogeology, he participated in and presided over geological investigations and related issues of numerous large and medium-sized hydraulic and hydropower projects in the Yangtze River basin, such as the preliminary design of the Wujiangdu Project, the study of the regional tectonic stability of the Danjiangkou Project, the early investigation of the head of the Taocha Canal of South-North Water Diversion, and the dam site comparison of the Wan'an Hydropower Station.

During the design and construction of the Gezhouba Dam project, Chen Deji studied major geological problems of the Gezhouba Dam project, including weak intercalated interlayer, the fault structure of the riverbed, and the high permeable zone. Since 1977, he served as the professional technical director of the geology of the design contractor of the Three Gorges Project, dedicating all his efforts to leading and organizing the investigation and research of the project as well as joining in its demonstration. He directly organized and participated in compiling the geological report on the comparison between the Sandouping Dam site and the Taipingxi Dam site of the Three Gorges Project and the geological report on the preliminary design of the scheme of water storage level. After the project's kickoff, he arranged the construction geological work during the initial stage of construction with

Wan'an Hydropower Station

the design and geological personnel stationed at the site. During the excavation of the foundations of various buildings in the Three Gorges Project, in response to major geological problems that may arise during the construction and operation of the main project, Chen Deji used more than ten geological and surveying technical methods to track and solve construction geological problems in a timely manner, providing reliable technical support for the smooth construction and operational safety of the project and making important contributions to the construction of the Three Gorges Project.

As an engineering geology expert, Chen Deji participated in technical discussions, consultation, review, and acceptance of many large-scale projects in China, such as the prediction of the Xin Tan landslide, the foundation survey of Shenzhen Airport Road, and the regulation survey of Huanglashi landslide, all of which achieved great social and economic benefits.

Chen Deji was awarded the "Chinese Engineering Survey Master" in 1990 and the "Young and Middle-aged Experts with Outstanding Contribution" in 1991. In the same year, he was awarded the special allowance of the State Council and the "National Outstanding Science and Technology Worker" in 1997.

XU RUICHUN

"The King of Qing River" Who Conducted Investigation His Whole Life

Between June and December 1956, Xu Ruichun heard about China's plan to build a dam on the Three Gorges of the Yangtze River while interning in Beibei, Chongqing Province. With full ambition at the time, he chose the Yangtze River as his assignment after graduation. He vowed to serve his country and the people by applying his intelligence in the hydraulic construction of the Yangtze River. At the graduation symposium, Xu Ruichun, usually a man of few words, took over the podium to reveal his desire to participate in constructing the Three Gorges Project on the Yangtze River. He said, "The era of Columbus's discovery of the New World has ended. But right under our feet, deep in the earth, there are still many mysteries waiting for us to uncover. The construction of the Yangtze River water conservancy and hydropower project calls for the younger generation, so let's give our alma mater more reports of victory with practical action!"

XU RUICHUN, born in 1936, was from Nahe, Heilongjiang Province. He was a member of the CPC and a national engineering survey master. He served as the chief engineer of the Three Gorges Survey and Design Institute of the Yangtze River Conservancy Commission and the deputy chief engineer of its Comprehensive Survey Bureau.

Xu Ruichun (second from left) at work

Xu Ruichun graduated from the Department of Hydrology and Engineering Geology of Northeast Institute of Geology (now Changchun University of Science and Technology) in 1956. After graduation, Xu Ruichun came a long way from the Northeast Plain to the Yangtze River and joined the survey team of the Yangtze River Basin Planning Office with great enthusiasm. He joined the comprehensive survey team of Jinsha River, thus starting his investigation career where he surveyed along high mountains and valleys, swift currents, and dangerous reefs, and worked under wind, snow and rain, thunder and lightning. He later surveyed the Jinsha River on site twice and dedicated his youth to the preliminary survey of several hydropower junctions on the upper reaches of the Yangtze River.

During the construction of the Gezhouba Dam project, Xu Ruichun took up the heavy burden and rose to the challenge. As the main geological technical director of the project, he was fully involved and led the investigation and construction geology of the Gezhouba Dam project. He conducted in-depth research on the issue of the "weak intercalated interlayer of the dam base" of project life regarding the geology of the Gezhouba Dam project. In order to solve the shear zone problem of the dam foundation, he led the survey geology team to spend more than two years thoroughly investigating the 72 layers of the interlayer shear zone under the base of Gezhouba Dam and proposed the construction, classification, and spatial distribution law of shear zone layer. The breakthrough of this major technical problem provided a scientific basis for site design and design optimization, which played an important role in solving the foundation treatment problem of the construction of Gezhouba Dam.

Xu Ruichun participated in and presided over the geological survey and construction geology of hydraulic and hydropower projects such as Geheyan, Gaobazhou, and Shuibuya. While constructing Shuibuya, the highest concrete-faced rockfill dam project in China then, he successfully solved complex environmental geological problems. He led and presided over the research of more than 170 landslides and dangerous rock mass in three large reservoirs of the Qing River, contributing to landslide treatment and migrant resettlement. The eight major topics of basic geological research of the Qing River Basin, which he planned, organized, led, and joined, were all leading domestically in the field of basic geological research of the basin.

From 1993 to 2000, Xu Ruichun concurrently served as the head of the Qing River Geological Brigade of the Yangtze River Conservancy Commission and was later appointed as the chief geological engineer of the Qing River Basin. He climbed all over the mountains along the Qingjiang River and thoroughly investigated the geological structure of the three dam sites of Qing River Geheyan, Gaobazhou, and Shuibuya. With the support of his survey results, the builders of the Qing River first completed the Diheyan Dam, then the Gaobazhou, and finally the Shuibuya. The hydropower development of the Qing River Basin made proud achievements. Xu Ruichun was thus praised as the "King of Qing River" in the hydraulic development and construction of the Qing River.

Xu Ruichun's masterpiece *Red Bed and Large Dams* systematically collected domestic and international examples of dams built on the red layer, comprehensively analyzed the geological problems that could arise in dam construction, and proposed solutions to these problems with real project examples, enriching China's treasure house of hydraulic and hydropower engineering geology.

Xu Ruichun successively won the gold investigation award of National Major Projects, the National Project Investigation Gold Award, and the gold award of the sixth National Project Investigation Excellence Award. In 2004, he was awarded the "National Engineering Investigation Master."

XU LINXIANG

A Master of Breaking Grounds in Water Conservancy

Xu Linxiang always put the demand of people in first place. When he needed to choose between the return ticket and the task of reservoir inspection of the earthquake-stricken areas, he resolutely decided to stay in the disaster area to continue working. Xu Linxiang said, "I'd like to spare no efforts to give back to the Yangtze River and the people. As an experienced hydraulic professional who worked in water conservancy for my whole life, when 300 million cubic meters of water was threatening the lives of millions of people, I should stay and use the many years of experience I accumulated in the practice of river regulation to contribute my part to protect the people in the disaster area from a second disaster.

Xu Linxiang, born in 1937, was a native of Jiaxing, Zhejiang Province, and a national engineering design master.

He graduated from Tsinghua University in 1959 with a degree in hydraulic structures. He became the chief engineer of the Changjiang Institute of Survey, Planning, Design, and Research of the Yangtze River Conservancy Commission in 1994.

In the 1960s, Xu Linxiang was responsible for the reinforcement design of the Danjiangkou Dam during the experimental study of its reinforcement treatment. He applied reinforcement measures such as cement grouting and backfilling of the concrete pit for penetrating cracks, which enabled the Danjiangkou Dam to meet the requirements of the design standards. In the 1970s, in the experimental study of clayey siltstone

Xu Linxiang

and weak intercalated interlayer of the Gezhouba hydropower project, Xu Linxiang was responsible for designing the foundation treatment of the Erjiang sluice, which successfully solved the foundation treatment problem of building a large sluice on a weak intercalated interlayer. It was his experience that led to the dam construction on the "red bed" and the treatment of the weak intercalated interlayer in the dam foundation rock mass.

In 1985, Xu Linxiang led and presided over the design of a new type of gravity arch dam at Geheyan. He overcame the difficulties of outdated software and hardware facilities with his team then, solving problems including the stress of the arch dam, the stability of the arch support on the second bank, and the slope stability. He successfully designed a new type of gravity arch dam with gravity top, arch bottom, and different grouting processes, which endured the over-storage water level in the reservoir in 1998. This novel dam type filled the blank in China's dam design and won the gold award of the Excellent Engineering Design Award of the Ministry of Water Resources and the gold award of the Eighth National Excellent Engineering Design Award.

Since 1991, Xu Linxiang had presided over the preliminary design of the Gaobazhou Water Hydropower Project as the technical leader of the design institute, making decisions on major technical issues. The project adopted more advanced technologies in the design of the dam structure layout, energy dissipation scheme, RCC cofferdam, spiral case, etc., which saved tens of millions of yuan in cost, shortened the linear construction duration by

Geheyan Hydropower Project

nearly ten months, and guaranteed the realization of the goal of water storage and power generation in advancement. The dam withstood the test of the 1998 catastrophic flood and the over-storage water level of the reservoir. The project design won the gold award of Excellent Engineering Design Award from both Ministry of Water Resources and the state.

In 1994, as the chief engineer of the design institute, Xu Linxiang started presiding over the hydraulic part of the technical design, bidding design, and construction detail design of the Three Gorges Project. He led the project "Key Technology Research on Steep and High Slopes of Three Gorges Locks," which successfully solved the problems of slope stability and the utilization of middle frusta in the design of high slopes of locks, saving large amounts of project investment compared to the preliminary design, and was evaluated as "advanced international level" during the acceptance.

During his water conservancy career, Xu Linxiang designed projects from scratch and improved and reinforced designs that transformed the projects. He made significant contributions to the safe operation and risk prevention of the completed Danjiangkou Dam, Gezhouba Dam, Geheyan dam, Gaobazhou Dam, and many more water conservancy projects.

LEI ZHIDONG

Who Cared about Tsinghua University and Furthered
Tian Shan's Development through Rivers

The first time Lei Zhidong returned from Xinjiang, he was already worried about the water resources there. He was busy helping sick teachers and cleaning toilets for students with his colleagues. He always thought about "assisting young people in making some achievement" after becoming an academician ... When Lei Zhidong was serving as the head of the Department of Water Resources at Tsinghua University. During the 1990s, it was popular to study abroad. At that time, he set three goals for his tenure: to attract more graduates to work in the national water resources department, to help young teachers grow faster, and to improve the department's school-running conditions. It was so moving, considering how bright and relaxing his laugh always was in contrast to the heavy burden shown in these three goals.

LEI ZHIDONG (1938–2015), a native of Li County, Hunan Province, was a member of the Chinese Communist Party, an expert in farmland irrigation and water resources, an educator of hydraulic engineering, and an academician of the Chinese Academy of Engineering. He graduated with a bachelor's degree from the Department of Water Resources of Tsinghua University in 1960 and a master's degree in 1965, after which he stayed to teach.

Lei Zhidong

Lei Zhidong was mainly engaged in basic research on soil water, four-water (atmospheric water, surface water, soil water, groundwater) transformation, and farmland irrigation and hydrological water resources. He applied them to water-saving irrigation and rational allocation and utilization of water resources in irrigation areas. His book, *Soil Hydrodynamics*, won the first prize in the Outstanding Scientific and Technological Book Award of the Ministry of Water Resources.

Lei Zhidong has conducted groundbreaking research in soil water and farmland irrigation over the years, innovated water operation models and made important contributions to furthering domestic research on soil water issues and the development of farmland irrigation disciplines. While engaging in theoretical research, he had always been working on the frontier, traveling all over the arid and semi-arid areas in the north. He conducted more in-depth research on scientific evaluation and rational utilization of groundwater resources.

Lei Zhidong had long been working closely with mega irrigation districts such as Yarkant in Xinjiang, Qingtongxia in Ningxia, and Weishan in Shandong, carrying out on-site monitoring experiments, the renovation planning of water conservation in the irrigation district, water use management, and the informatization construction of irrigation, and dedicating his energy and efforts to the improvement of water resources in these irrigation districts. Based on the characteristics of irrigation areas in arid and semi-arid regions, he proposed analytical ideas and methods for balancing water resources and salt, which were of great value in theory and application.

In 1992, Lei Zhidong led his team to Xinjiang and made the visionary decision to carry out hydrological and water resources research there. In about six years, he not only established a water and salt monitoring system in the oasis irrigation area with his team but also studied the process and mechanism of the consumption of local water resources and the three destinations of salt in the oasis irrigation area as well as established a four-water transformation model for the oasis irrigation area in the arid area. More importantly, while compiling *The Plan of Support Facilities Installation and Water-saving Reconstruction of Yarkant River Irrigation District*, the original proposal was to expand the irrigation area. Later, they applied the research results of "four-water transformation" and conducted an analysis of the impact of irrigation area expansion on ecology, based on which they proposed the measures to reduce 1.4 million mu of land reclamation (one mu is about 666.7 square meters). The new proposal saved more than 10 million yuan in reclamation costs and maintained the natural ecology.

With the support of the science and technology project of the national "Ninth Five-Year Plan," Lei led a team to study the regulation and ecological environmental protection of the mainstem of the Tarim River, analyzed the trend changes in the annual water volume of the source and mainstem from 1955 to 1995, and proposed the water balance of the mainstem, the conversion consumption model of water resources, and the allocation scheme of water resources of the mainstem, which had become a preliminary task of "The Recent Comprehensive Regulation of Tarim River" project that was approved and invested by the State Council. In 2002, he was awarded the second prize in the State Science and Technology Advancement Award for his work *Research on the Relationship of Four Water Conversion in the Yarkant River Plain Oasis* and *Research on the Regulation and Ecological Environmental Protection of the Tarim River Mainstem*.

WU ZHONGRU

The Guardian of Dam Safety

During the era of wars, Wu Zhongur's family was searched many times by Japanese soldiers because his parents covered the anti-Japanese guerrillas many times. Thus, his father had no choice but to take his mother, who was pregnant at the time, to hide all across Lake Tai until he was born that fall in the dense reeds. During his childhood, his father rowed a small boat across Lake Tai to hide him from the Japanese army. Whenever he recalled his childhood full of difficulties, Wu Zhongyu would sigh with emotion, "My childhood was spent during two wars, so I always had a sense of responsibility and mission to combine my career with the prosperity of my country."

Wu Zhongru, born in 1939, was a native of Yixing, Jiangsu Province. He was a member of the Chinese Communist Party, an expert in hydraulic structures, an academician of the Chinese Academy of Engineering, and a professor and doctoral supervisor at Hohai University.

Wu Zhongru

After graduating from the East China Institute of Water Conservancy (now Hohai University) in 1963 with a hydraulic engineering major, Wu Zhongru successively worked at the Hydrology Institute of China Institute of Water Resources and Hydropower Research and the North Henan Experimental Station. From 1969 to 1975, he worked at the Tieshan Reservoir in Jiyuan City, Henan Province, and the Bureau of Power Industry in the Xinxiang region. From 1975 to 1979, he served at the leading group of power plant construction development in Xuzhou, Jiangsu Province. In 1979, he served as a professor and the director of the Academic Committee at Hohai University. He joined the Communist Party of China in 1986 and was elected as an academician of the Chinese Academy of Engineering in 1997.

Wu Zhongru had long been engaging in teaching and research in the field of hydraulic structures and dam safety monitoring and surveillance. He built a safety protection system for large Chinese dams.

Wu Zhongru was the first internationally to propose comprehensive field data and formulate deformation monitoring indicators using the small probability method, viscoelasticity, and viscoelastic-plastic theory. These research results have been applied in almost all dam projects in China, including the Three Gorges Dam, guarding the safety of every dam all the time.

Wu Zhongru first proposed and developed an expert system for comprehensive evaluation of dam safety. The system consisted of "one engine and four libraries" (inference, knowledge library, data library, method library, photo library). It fully utilized artificial intelligence technology, applied, and developed the advanced hardware and software of modern computers, conducted whole-course comprehensive analysis, evaluation, and decision-making aiding dam safety, and played an important role in real-time monitoring of dam safety.

Wu Zhongru developed a complete dam monitoring model system, proposed and established deterministic, hybrid models, and monitoring mathematical forecasting models based on chaos theory, fuzzy mathematics, gray systems, and neural networks, which were widely applied in dam monitoring. He developed and perfected the theory and method of back analysis, reversed deformation, thermodynamics, fracture, infiltration, and other physical and mechanical parameters combining field data and theoretical analysis. His theories and techniques had significant theoretical and practical value for perfecting the dam engineering theory and improving the accuracy of numerical models.

Wu Zhongru cultivated a large batch of talents who were active hydraulic professionals. He taught postgraduate students lessons such as "Safety Monitoring Theory and Its Application in Hydraulic Structures" and "Expert System of Comprehensive Evaluation of Dam Safety." Many of his students have become key personnel in the teaching, researching, and designing of hydraulics and hydropower in China.

Wu Zhongru has won many national and provincial (ministerial) science and technology advancement awards. "Research on Mathematical Model of Concrete Dam Deformation Observation and its Application: Safety Monitoring and Forecasting" won the third prize in the National Science and Technology Advancement Award in 1990. "High Dam Safety Monitoring Technology and its Feedback" (Wu was responsible for researching four of the seven sub-topics) won the second prize in the National Science and Technology Advancement Award in 1995. "Theory and Method of Dam and Dam Foundation Safety Monitoring and its Applied Research" won the second prize in the State Science and Technology Advancement Award in 2004. "Research on Detection of Accident Potential and Health Diagnosis of Major Concrete Hydraulic Structures" won the second prize in the State's Science and Technology Advancement Award in 2007.

ZHENG SHOUREN

The Kind Master Who Was Called
"The Academician at the Construction Site"

For over 50 years, Zheng Shouren has never forgotten his original intention and always practiced his vow when joining the Party. He put the interests of the Party, the country, and the people above all else. He has been known as the "academician at the construction site" for living on sites for many years. He insisted on being on duty on holidays such as Spring Festival and National Day. After his cancer diagnosis, he still insisted on working during his treatment and worked overload with high intensity all year round. Whenever a flood or other natural disaster occurred, he always took the lead in making donations and only left the name of "Yangtze River Conservancy Commission employee" on the remittance bill. Most of his earnings through writing and lecturing were used for collective welfare undertakings or donated to colleagues with difficult living conditions.

ZHENG SHOUREN (1940–2020) was a native of Yingshang, Anhui Province. He was a member of the Chinese Communist Party, an expert in hydraulic and hydropower engineering, and an academician of the Chinese Academy of Engineering. He served as the chief engineer of the Yangtze River Conservancy Commission and the director of the Survey and Design Representative Office of the Three Gorges Project.

Zheng Shouren

Zheng Shouren was born in a small town by the Huai River in Yingshang County, Anhui Province. As a child, he witnessed and experienced the destruction of the Huai River floods and thus aspired to become a hydraulic engineer when he grew up.

In 1958, Zheng Shouren was admitted into the Department of Hydropower Station and Hydraulic Engineering of the East China Institute of Water Conservancy (now Hohai University). In 1963, Zheng Shouren and other young people came to the Lushui Puqi Hydropower Station after graduating from university, where they were trained and sharpened at the test dam site of the Three Gorges. He also became prepared to show his talents by working on all the great rivers of China. Due to his outstanding performance, he joined the Communist Party of China honorably at Lu Shuipuqi, which was under busy construction.

In 1969, Zheng Shouren was appointed as the head of the diversion major group of the survey and design brigade Wujiangdu, presiding over the design of the diversion and cofferdam. In this project, he successfully designed the first concrete arch cofferdam of underwater construction in China, which became the first milestone of his career in water conservancy.

Zheng Shouren joined the construction of Gezhouba Dam in 1974. He successfully built the longitudinal earth-rock cofferdam in the Yangtze River with a force-resisting design "guard the points and lines," which was also applied to the earth and rock cofferdam design of the first phase of the Three Gorges Project. He presided over the river interception and the second phase of cofferdam design. He proposed a "reinforced stone cage" as the scheme for protecting the dam bottom with closure, which significantly reduced the losses of advanced cast materials. He completed the historical task of river interception and was awarded the National Design Excellence Award. The Erjiang and Sanjiang projects of Gezhouba Dam won the Grand Prize in the State Science and Technology Advancement Award.

The river interception of the Three Gorges Project

In 1986, he served as the deputy chief engineer of the Yangtze River Basin Planning Office and the director of the Geheyan Design Representative Division, turning the Geheyan Hydropower Dam, which was standing upright in the clear blue river, into China's first composite dam with gravity top and arch bottom, into one of the "five golden flowers" of hydropower construction at the time. The project won the gold award in the National Excellent Engineering Design Award.

In 1994, the Three Gorges Project entered the construction stage. From the first phase of the project, marked by the completion of the interception of the river, to the second phase of the project, marked by the power generation from the left bank power plant and the navigation of the permanent locks, and eventually to the third phase of the project, marked by the comprehensive power generation from all units and the full completion of construction, Zheng Shouren took full responsibility for the construction of this world's largest hydraulic project. He served as the director and chief engineer of the Investigation and Design Representative Bureau of the Three Gorges Project, presiding over the research and solution of all design-related engineering technical issues during the construction process. In 1997, the river interception of the Three Gorges Project was completed. The project was awarded the gold award of the National Design Excellence Award and the first prize of the State Science and Technology Advancement Award for its technical achievements, ranking among the world's top ten technological achievements in 1997.

Zheng Shouren was awarded as an excellent communist party member many times and a special model worker of the Ministry of Hydropower and the Ministry of Water Resources twice. In 1989, he was awarded the title of "National Advanced Worker" by the State Council. In 1994, he was awarded the title of "Young and Middle-aged Experts with Outstanding Contributions" by the Ministry of Personnel. He was awarded the title of "Special Contributor to the Geheyan Project" and "Excellent Builder of the Three Gorges Project." He also won the Lifetime Achievement Award of the International Commission on Large Dams. In 2019, he was awarded the "New China Most Beautiful Striver Award" ... He was known as the "Contemporary Emperor Yu," the "Backbone of the Three Gorges," and the "Cornerstone of Large Dams."

ZHANG CHAORAN

A Practitioner of "Three Gorges Spirit"

Zhang Chaoran studied professional technology diligently, stuck to principles, stayed away from fame and fortune, and chose to support the water conservancy construction in the west without hesitation. He interpreted the spirit of science with his own words and actions. He made outstanding contributions to the construction of projects such as the Three Gorges Project, Xiluodu Dam, Xiangjiaba dam, Baihetan Dam, and Wudongde Dam. He often said that to be a chief engineer is to be able to take responsibility. This was a manifestation of the great importance he placed on the responsibility and resolution of his work. He shaped and practiced the "Three Gorges Spirit," dedicated to his motherland's rivers regardless of the rewards, and witnessed the milestones of hydropower development in China.

ZHANG CHAORAN, born in Wenzhou, Zhejiang Province, in 1940, was a member of the Chinese Communist Party, an expert in hydraulic and hydropower engineering, and an academician of the Chinese Academy of Engineering. He graduated from the Department of Hydraulic Engineering of Tsinghua University. He served as the director of the Science and Technology Committee of China Three Gorges Corporation and the chief engineer of the design of Ertan Hydropower Station, the Chengdu Survey and Design Institute, and the China Three Gorges Project Corporation.

Zhang Chaoran

At the time of graduation assignment, Zhang Chaoran gave up on the generous package offered by higher education institutions and the Chinese Academy of Engineering. He resolutely chose to go to the west and dedicate himself to the water conservancy construction in the west. Since then, he has accompanied the great rivers of the motherland for more than 50 years. The sum of installed hydropower capacity of projects he presided over or constructed accounted for 1/3 of the country's total capacity.

In 1996, Zhang Chaoran became the chief engineer of China Three Gorges Project Corporation. Upon he took office, he studied the Three Gorges Project in detail and spent nearly a month sorting out his thoughts. He understood that the Three Gorges Project collected many years of scientific research achievements in China. He can only take real responsibility of the project by fully digesting the project materials.

When he was the chief engineer, Zhang Chaoran strictly controlled the quality standard and enforced the standards, always putting quality in the first place and doing his best for the Three Gorges Project. He carefully verified every data point and provided basis for every proposal with informative data and cases. Through unremitting efforts, he and other researchers eventually overcame technical problems one by one, contributing hard work and wisdom to ensure the construction quality of the Three Gorges Project, which was believed to be "a crucial strategy for a millennium to come where the national fortune lies."

The Three Gorges Project

After the initial operation of the Three Gorges project succeeded, Zhang Chaoran devoted into the construction of Xiluodu and Xiangjiaba hydropower station projects. For nearly ten years, he went back and forth between the Three Gorges on Yangtze River and Jinsha River, until Luoxidu and Xiangjiaba hydropower stations were fully put into operation in 2014. After that, Zhang Chaoran again committed himself to the hydropower construction of Jinsha River. Considering the problems in the construction, he was up for the challenge, looked up a lot of information, and continued to contribute his efforts in the hydropower construction.

Zhang Chaoran's meticulous, diligent and earnest work spirit was also reflected in his work notes, the "book." Stacks of "books" consisted of Zhang Chaoran's work notes for many years, which was covered with all kinds of project data in a neat and tidy format and accumulated a huge amount of "big data" over time, which became the most valuable first-hand information for his in-depth analysis, research, and timely control over the dam construction and operation status.

Zhang Chaoran spent his life with rivers, dedicating himself to hydropower undertakings and working at the front line with pragmatic and meticulous attitude. He was the practitioner of the "Three Gorges Spirit" and the shaper of the "Three Gorges Spirit."

MA HONGQI

Who Devoted Himself to River Regulation for Half of a Century

Ma Hongqi was a simple and kind elder, who firmly believed in responsibility and dedication, and worked with the mountains and rivers as the industry leader for a long time. He was not afraid of hardship and was bold to innovate. His project portfolio included countless power stations, creating the bright electric sparkles in the valleys. In many people's opinion, hydraulic and hydropower work is profound, boring and hard. But Ma Hongqi never got tired and frequently obtained great achievements in this field.

MA HONGQI, born in Shanghai in 1942, was a member of the Chinese Communist Party, an expert in hydraulic and hydropower construction, and an academician of the Chinese Academy of Engineering. He was a graduate of the Department of Water Resources of Tsinghua University, a senior consultant of Huaneng Lancang River Hydropower Inc., a chief engineer and director of the Sinohydro Bureau 14 Co., Ltd, and a chief engineer of the Lancang River Hydropower Co.; he also won the Lifetime Achievement Award of the International Commissions on Large Dams.

Ma Hongqi

In 1967, at 25, Ma Hongqi came to Yunnan Province all by himself. He said, "Yunnan is rich in hydropower resources. As hydropower professionals, we should stay close to the rivers." In 1989, at the age of 47, Ma Hongqi was involved in leading the construction of the Guangzhou Pumped Storage Power Station, the world's largest pumped storage power station and the first in China. In 2001, at 59, Ma Hongqi devoted himself to the construction of the Xiaowan Hydropower Station, rated as the most difficult hydropower station to build in the world at the time. He studied the complex geological conditions, challenged cutting-edge technical problems and pushed the world's arch dams to reach the 300 meters grade.

Ma Hongqi has been engaged in hydraulic and hydropower engineering construction for 54 years. He started as a front-line worker in hydropower stations, joined and presided over the construction of more than 30 large hydropower projects, successfully overcoming many world-class major technical problems in high dam construction, underground engineering, and high dam navigation. He has thus become a leading figure in promoting China's hydraulic and hydropower engineering technology to reach international leading level.

In the aspect of high arch dam construction, Ma Hongqi worked on the major technical issues of Xiaowan Hydropower Station collectively with his colleagues, established a key technology system for ultra-high arch dams, and led the construction of high arch dams to reach 300-meter level. Xiaowan Hydropower Station was awarded the International Milestone Project Award, the gold award of the

National Quality Engineering Award, and the China Civil Engineering Zhan Tianyou Award. His research results was widely applied to construct high arch dams such as Jinping Grade I Hydropower Station, Xiluodu Hydropower Station, and Baihetan Hydropower Station.

In the aspect of safety construction of high earth and rock dams, Ma Hongqi successfully developed the "Digital Dam" system for the first time, a significant innovation of dam construction quality control technology internationally. The research results have been successfully applied in the construction of high earth and rock dams such as Lianghekou, Shuangjiangkou, and Changhe Dam.

In terms of the construction of high RCC dams, Ma Hongqi developed and completed an intelligent control and management information system of construction quality, which was successfully applied to Huangdeng RCC dam in China (203 meters high), the highest RCC in China. It advanced the compacted concrete dam technology to a new level.

In terms of high dam navigation technology, relying on the construction of Jinghong ship lift, Ma Hongqi led the team to invent a hydraulic boat lift that uses hydropower as lifting power and safety measures. The technology was rated as an important milestone in the history of ship lifter, through which China-invented hydraulic type ship lifter broke through the technical bottleneck of

Xiaowan Hydropower Station

traditional ship lifter theoretically with more technical advantages. The achievement was awarded the State Technological Innovation Award.

In the aspect of underground engineering, Ma Hongqi proposed the basic principle of construction planning for underground cavern clusters and five key technologies for safe construction, which achieved safe and high-quality construction of projects and were commonly adopted in other projects.

GAO ANZE

Who Spared No Efforts to Devote to the People

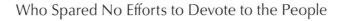

Gao Anze always kept the well-beings of the people in his heart. He believed that the interests of the people are always critical. He dedicated to his job and took each project seriously and diligently. Just as he wrote in his application for CPC membership, under all circumstances, I need to put the interests of the party and the people above all. Personal interests should be subordinated to the interests of the party, for which I need to take more responsibility and complete more work with higher difficulty than non-party comrades, or even sacrifice everything including my own life, if necessary.

GAO ANZE, born in 1942, was a native of Yueqing, Zhejiang Province who graduated from Tsinghua University. He was a member of the Chinese Communist Party, a Chinese engineering design master, and a former chief engineer of the Ministry of Water Resources.

Gao Anze

Comrade Gao Anze had long been engaging in hydraulic and hydropower work. For decades, he always put the interests of the Party and the people above all else and made outstanding contributions to water conservancy and hydropower construction, for which he won the "Excellent Communist Party Member" title awarded by the State Organs Working Committee of the CPC Central Committee twice.

Shortly after graduating with his master's degree, Gao Anze took over the responsibility of leading the hydraulic engineering design of the preliminary design of the Ertan Hydropower Station. During the process, Gao Anze personally designed the software model, derived the required formulas, and stayed in the computer room all day long. His colleagues at Chengdu Survey and Design Institute commented, "President Gao almost put his life at risk for the Ertan project." The design of Ertan Hydropower Station completed under the leadership of Gao Anze was well received by experts and scholars and won the first prize of the Excellent Design Award of Ministry of Hydropower. He supported and participated in the compilation of "Test load method procedure of parabolic double-curvature arch dam," which won the first prize of the Excellent Design Award of the former General Administration of Hydropower.

Gao Anze participated in the planning of many hydropower projects in China and was involved in organizing the review of major problems and countermeasures of the Yellow River, water resources planning of the capital, ecological and environmental problems and its countermeasures of the Tarim River in Xinjiang, national water resources protection planning, and flood control construction opinions of the Nen River, Liao River, Lake Tai, Huai River, and Pearl River Basin. He presided over the redemonstration of the environmental evaluation of the Zipingpu Hydropower Station of the Min River in Sichuan. He also participated in the safety appraisal of reservoirs such as Beijing Ming Tombs Pumped Storage Power Station and the Yellow River Lijiaxia Hydropower Station before storage, the organization of the compilation of the hydraulic special planning of the Tenth Five-Year National Flood Control Plan, the organization of the compilation of the South-North Water Diversion Project, the technical pre-acceptance of the Three Gorges Phase II Project, and the quality inspection of the Three Gorges Phase III Project.

Gao Anze focused on investigation and research and was highly responsible to the people. He conducted in-depth field investigations, compiled and reviewed more than 40 flood control plans and water resource plans for the Yellow River, Huai River, Hai River, Lake Tai, Nen River, Songhua River, Hei River, and Ta River. He organized 13 major special studies to solve the water shortage problem in the northern region and more than ten preliminary tasks for the project of diverting Yellow River water to Tianjin, laying a good foundation for the modernization of water conservancy in the new era.

Yalong River Ertan Hydropower Station

CHEN ZUYU

Who Attended to Map the Mountains and Rivers Personally

Since 1992, Chen Zuyu had been working tirelessly for hosting an international landslide conference in China. He successively went to New Zealand and the United Kingdom to participate in the bidding process. After two unsuccessful bids, Chen Zuyu embarked on the journey again in 2004 and finally succeeded in applying for the hosting right of the Tenth International Landslide Conference. He said excitedly, "The engineering geology and geotechnical engineering communities in China had finally fulfilled a 12-year-long dream. Looking into the northern sky, I feel proud and honored for the great motherland!"

CHEN ZUYU, born in Chongqing in 1943, was an expert in hydraulic, hydropower and civil engineering. He was an academician of the Chinese Academy of Sciences and a professor-level senior engineer of the China Institute of Water Resources and Hydropower Research.

In 1966, Chen Zuyu graduated from the Department of Water Resources of Tsinghua University. After graduation, he engaged in the design of foundation treatment and reservoirs at the frontier of hydraulic and hydropower field in China. In 1979, as one of the first visiting scholars in China, he went to study at the University of Alberta in Canada under the supervision of Professor Morgenstern, a renowned geotechnical expert. During his two years of overseas study, he audited all graduate

Chen Zuyu

courses of the geotechnical major of the department of civil engineering. After returning to China in 1981, he joined the China Institute of Water Resources and Hydropower Research.

Chen Zuyu refined the theory and analytical calculation methods of the well-known Morgenstern-Price method in the field of slope stability analysis early in his career. His main contribution was to achieve important improvements to the mathematical-mechanical expression and theoretical connotation of this method, to provide the analytical solution of the equation of force and moment balance, and to put forward the boundary conditions required for solving this equation based on the principle of shear stress pairing. He derived the differential equations of soil force and moment balance with strict analytical methods and obtained closed-form solutions. He derived the formulas for the derivatives required to solve the equations of forces and moment balance by Newton's method, which solved the problem of difficult convergence of numerical calculations that various rigorous methods of stability analysis failed to solve for a long time. He proposed the necessary boundary conditions to meet the assumption of lateral forces on soil stripes to ensure that the shear stress pairing principle is not damaged, and thus comprehensively improved the Morgenstern-Price method, which has an important academic status in the field of slope stability analysis.

Chen Zuyu always attached great importance to study and solve the anti-slide stability issues of structures and slope during project constructions while engaging in theoretical research. In 1989, a landslide occurred in the Tianshengqiao and Manwan hydropower stations, both under construction. As the main participant and person in charge of the key scientific research project of the Ministry of Electric Power, Chen Zuyu proposed correct measures for slope rescue and reinforcement based on a comprehensive analysis of the landslide mechanism, which saved the project from troubles and ensured its smooth progress.

Manwan Hydropower Station

Chen Zuyu had been going back and forth between landslides sites and hydropower construction sites for years. He visited the site in person and contributed his abundant knowledge to help solve difficult problems when Hancheng Reservoir, Manwan Dam, Tianshengqiao-II Dam, Ertan Hydropower Station, Tianhuangping Dam, Dashuigou Dam, and E'tan Dam were facing landslide hazards. He was a member of the expert group for dam safety appraisal of the Three Gorges, Xiaolangdi, Lijiaxia, Dongfeng, Baozhuji, Xucun, Zipingpu, and other large water conservancy projects.

Since 1998, as a member of the Supervision Mission of World Bank's Yangtze River Levee Reinforcement Project, he visited the site nine times to inspect the design and construction quality. In engineering consultation, he fully applied his creative theoretical achievements and rich experience in scientific research to solve difficult problems in project decision making. For example, he applied his findings on the two possibilities of the Sarma method's ignorance of the direction of inter-bar forces to rectify an incorrect conclusion in the anti-slide stability of the three dam sections of the Three Gorges Project. He applied his research results on earth pressure and three-dimensional analysis to demonstrate the feasibility of the hybrid dam of Yixing Pumped Storage Power Station.

BIBLIOGRAPHY

Anonymous. "A Tribute to Wang Wenshao: The Founder of Geodynamics and Geotechnical Seismic Research in China." Accessed on April 18th, 2021. http://www.chincold.org.cn/chincold/zt/ccqb/ccqb/webinfo/2018/06/1528341983916394.htm.

Anonymous. "Academician Lu Yaoru Donated 3.6 Million Yuan to Establish the 'Ecological Environment and Geological Engineering Incentive Fund.'" Accessed on April 20th, 2021. https://news.tongji.edu.cn/info/1002/69289.htm.

Anonymous. "Academician Zhang Chuhan: Safety Is the Foundation of Hydropower Station Operation." Accessed on April 20th. http://www.hydropower.org.cn/showNewsDetail.asp?nsId=4044.

Anonymous. "Lifelong Efforts in the Geotechnical Field: Academician Ge Xiurun, (III)." *Geotechnical Engineering Journal* 6, no. 32 (2013): 1297–1298.

Anonymous. "Mao Zhi: A Farmland Irrigation Expert with Global Reputation." Accessed on April 18th, 2021. http://swrh.whu.edu.cn/rwzf/20170908/4398.html.

Anonymous. "Senior Academician Cao Chusheng Spent His 90th Birthday Sharing His Life Experiences with Students." Accessed on April 20th, 2021. http://jgxy.tju.edu.cn/info/1074/1869.htm.

Anonymous. "Shi Jiayang: A Great Teacher Who Specialized in Both Teaching and Research." *Hebei Water Resources*, no. 8 (2017): 34.

Anonymous. "The Advanced Achievements of Comrades Cui Zhengquan." Accessed on April 20th, 2021. http://slwm.mwr.gov.cn/slkm/200909/t20090922_1102.html.

Anonymous. "The Model of Party Members, the Style of Master: the Advanced Achievements of Comrade Cui Zhengquan." Accessed on April 18th, 2021. http://www.chinawater.com.cn/ztgz/xwzt/2007ymkm/3/200707/t20070704_133260.htm.

Anonymous. "Xu Linxiang: A Design Master Who 'Filled in the Blanks' for China's Water Conservancy Undertakings." Accessed on April 18th, 2021. http://www.chinawater.com.cn/wh/rw/slzsx/200506/t20050628_16645.htm.

Anonymous. "Zhang Chaoran: A Hydropower Career with Continuous Breakthroughs." Accessed on April 20th, 2021. http://www.hydropower.org.cn/showNewsDetail.asp?nsId=11999.

Anonymous. "Zheng Shouren, the 'Academician of the Site,' Who Spent His Life Guarding the Three Gorges Dam Passed Away." Accessed on April 20th, 2021. https://baijiahao.baidu.com/s?id=1673276116306099981&wfr=spider&for=pc.

Anonymous. "Zhexi Hydropower Station, Known as the First "Ruby" of Hunan Province with 105,000 Thousand Construction Workers and Nearly 140,000 Migrants Involved, Is Magnificent and Fascinating." Accessed on December 21st, 2021. https://view.inews.qq.com/a/20211229A09WJ200.

Bai, Ping. "Love for Rivers: Interview with Ma Hongqi, Academician of Chinese Academy of Engineering and Former Senior Advisor of Huaneng Lancang River Company." *China Energy*, no. 41 (2019): 25–27.

Baidu Baike. https://baike.baidu.com/.

Chen, Deji. *Crossing the Blue Hills Adds Nothing to One's Years: Selected Essays of Chen Deji*. Beijing: China Water Conservancy and Hydropower Publishing House, 2018.

Chen, Houqun. *The Autobiography of Chen Houqun: A Life of Chasing Dreams*. Beijing: Science Press, 2018.

Chen, Ling. "Zheng Zhaojing, Founder of Chinese Modern Water Conservancy Undertakings." *Archives and Development*, no. 2 (2014): 57–60.

Chen, Lingruo. "An Interview with Professor Qian Ning." *Chinese Water Conservancy*, no. 1 (1982): 46–47.

Chen, Ting and Wang Shen. "Dou Guoren: Ten Years in Soviet Union, a Lifetime of Achievement." Accessed on April 18th, 2021. http://news.sciencenet.cn/sbhtmlnews/2019/8/348358.shtm.

Chen, Zongliang. *Essays and Articles of Li E'Ding*. Beijing: China Electric Power Press, 2004.

Cheng, Hong. "Searching for Lu Xiaoyi, Who Returned to China on the Same Ship as Qian Xuesen." Accessed on April 18th, 2021. http://www.bj93.gov.cn/wyhc/hjjj/201505/t20150522_218314.htm.

Cheng, Xiaotao, Wang Lianxiang, Fan Zhao, et al. *A Wise Man Who Loved Water: The Biography of Lin Bingnan*. Beijing: China Science and Technology Press, 2014.

China Hydropower Engineering Society, China Electric Power Construction Group Limited, and SinoHydro Bureau 8 Co., Ltd. *The Academician Who Grew out of the Rivers: Essays and Articles of Tan Jingyi*. Beijing: China Water Conservancy and Hydropower Publishing House, 2017.

China Hydropower Engineering Society. *Essays and Articles of Luo Xibei* Beijing: China Electric Power Press, 2006.

China Institute of Hydrogeology and Engineering Geology Survey, Editorial Department of *China Karst*. "Deeply remembering Mr. Hu Haitao." *China Karst*, no. 4 (1998): 34.

China National Committee on Large Dams. "Academician Ma Hongqi of Huaneng Lancang River Hydropower Inc. won the Lifetime Achievement Award of International Commission on Large Dams." Accessed on April 18th, 2021. http://www.chincold.org.cn/chincold/news/webinfo/2019/06/19/1561955158951384.htm.

Dai, Yong, Wang Ping, and Jin Wenhua. *Exploring the Estuary and Studying the Coast: A Biography of Chen Jiyu*. Beijing: Shanghai Jiao Tong University Press, 2015.

Fu, Aiping and Li Guoqiang. "Consuming Himself and Lighting Others: Wang Sanyi, Former Chief Engineer of Central South Survey and Design Institute." *Trend in Hunan*, no. 1 (2005): 39–43.

Gao, Hong. *Li Yizhi, the Water Sage of One Generation* Beijing: Writers Publishing House, 2017.

He, Ping. "Xu Linxiang: The 72-year-old Engineering Design Master Who First Entered the Disaster Area." *Guangming Daily*, May 29th, 2008, 7.

Hou, Quanliang. "Li Fudu." *The World of Water Conservancy*, no. 6 (1990): 2.

Hu, Buchuan. *Chronology of Mr. Li Yizhi*. Nanjing: Hohai University Press.

Hu, Buchuan. *The Posthumous Works of Mr. Li Yizhi*. Nanjing: Hohai University Press, 2020.

Hu, Shixiang, Guan Wenlong, and Tang Hongwei. "Xie Shileng: The Prosperity of Ports." In "Selfless Dedication to the Motherland: Three Intellectuals Who Are Concerned about the Transportation Industry." *Guangming Daily*, December 23th, 2008, 7.

Huo, Zhongyi, Wang Jingrong, and Zheng Feimin. "Li Peicheng: Crossing the Blue Hills Adds Nothing to One's Years." *China Science News*, August 28th, 2017, 8.

Institute of Geology and Geophysics, and Chinese Academy of Sciences. *The Geological Career of Gu Dezhen*. Beijing: Geological Press, 2014.

Jia, Dan, and Rui Yuan. "The Persistent Pursuit of Qian Zhengjing." *Essay Compilation of CPC History*, no. 5 (2013): 27–30.

Jiang, Caihong. *Wen Fubo: The General Who Regulates Water*. Wuhan: Changjiang Publishing House, 2020.

Jin, Huaijuan and Chen Songping. *Zheng Shouren: The Son of Yangtze River*. Wuhan: Changjiang Publishing House, 2020.

Jin, Xiaoxia. "The Devotion of a Generation of Geologists (I): Remembering Lu Yaoru, Academician of Chinese Academy of Engineering." *China Disaster Reduction*, no. 7 (2011): 55–57.

Jin, Xiaoxia. "The Devotion of a Generation of Geologists (I): Remembering Lu Yaoru, Academician of Chinese Academy of Engineering." *China Disaster Reduction*, no. 9 (2011): 54–56.

Lai, Ying. "Keep One's Promise—Remembering Gao Anze, Director of General Institute of Hydropower Planning and Design, Ministry of Electricity." *Ziguang Pavillion*, no. 8 (1995): 28–29.

Li, Guoying. "Commemorating the Yellow River Elder Zhang Hanying; Promote the New Development of River Regulation." Accessed on April 18th, 2021. http://www.chinawater.com.cn/ztgz/hy/jnzhy/201005/t20100512_118761.htm.

Li, Huanzhang. *Wang Huayun and Xiaolangdi*. Zhengzhou: Yellow River Water Conservancy Press, 2015.

Li, Minquan and Wang Yue'e. "Crossing the Blue Hills Adds Nothing to One's Years, Visiting All Magnificent Mountains Creates One's New Vision: Remembering the National Engineering Survey Master Xu Ruichun." *China Three Gorges Project Development*, no. 2 (2007): 83–86.

Li, Rongqing and Yang Linhu. *A Life of Water Transport: Biography of Liu Jizhou*. Beijing: China Science and Technology Press, 2017.

Lin, Yishan. *Memoirs of Lin Yishan*. Wuhan: Changjiang Publishing House, 2019.

Liu, Dongmei and Sun Zhe. "Zhang Chuhan, an Academician of Chinese Academy of Sciences, an Expert in Hydraulic and Hydropower Engineering." *Beijing Education (Higher Education)*, no. 2 (2002): 1.

Liu, Fengcai. "The Long Journey Cannot Stop: Chen Mingzhi, an Academician of the Chinese Academy of Engineering." *Chinese Water Conservancy*, no. 12 (1996): 42–43.

Liu, Guowei. "Honest and Modest Personality: Remembering the Famous Hydraulic Expert, Academician Xu Qianqing." *Water Science Development* 1, no. 22 (2011): 147–150.

Liu, Hongwei. "Zhang Yong, Academician of Chinese Academy of Engineering and the Pioneer of Chinese Hydropower Energy Theory." *Science and Technology Innovation and Branding,* no. 10 (2014): 8–11.

Liu, Jun. *Cui Zhangsheng, the Guardian of Investigation*. Wuhan: Changjiang Publishing House, 2020.

Liu Suxia, Liang Jiyang, Liu Shuyong, et al. "For the Prosperity of Water." *China Science News*, March 19th, 2018: 8.

Liu, Suxia, Liu Shuyong, Wu Yongbao, et al. "For the Prosperity of Water: A Retrospective of the Early Study and Research Experiences of Hydrologist Liu Changming." Accessed on April 18th, 2021. http://news.sciencenet.cn/htmlnews/2018/3/406018.shtm.

Liu, Weihan. "Xukai: Non-stop Trickle." Accessed on April 18th, 2021. https://archives.hhu.edu.cn/2018/0528/c5352a172973/page.htm.

Liu, Weirong, Shi Xin. "The Hydraulic Engineering Who Loved the Land of Jiangsu and Huai River: Interview with Zhou Junliang, an Academician of Chinese Academy of Engineering and a 'Chinese Engineering Design Master.'" *Archives and Development*, no. 9 (1999): 14–15, 21.

Long, Zhangqing. "Academician Luo Shaoji, an Expert in Hydropower." *In the Same Boat*, no. 5 (2000): 49.

Lu, Shunmin. *Biography of Academician Zhu Bofang*. Beijing: China Electric Power Press, 2018.

Lu, Shunmin. *Biography of Pan Jiazheng*. Beijing: China Electric Power Press, 2016.

Lu, Youmei. "Building the Three Gorges for My Motherland." *Hubei Political News*, no. 3 (1994): 38.

Lv, Dongguang. "In Memory of Academician Zhao Guofan: The Master of the Civil Engineering Who Live on as a Model." Accessed on April 18th, 2021. http://news.sciencenet.cn/htmlnews/2017/2/368403.shtm.

Mao, Desun and Geng Dongcheng. "Qian Lingxi: A Pioneer in Computational Mechanics Engineering Structural

Optimization Design in China." Accessed on April 20th, 2021. https://www.cas.cn/zt/rwzt/2009yldqx/qian-lingxi/qlxjnwz/201003/t20100331_2810269.html.

Nanjing Hydraulic Research Institute. *Essays and Articles of Academician Xu Qianqing*. Beijing: China Electric Power Press, 2016.

Ning, Guiling, Kong Yanmei, and Gu Qian. "Qiu Dahong: A Relationship with the 'Sea.'" *Democracy and Science*, no. 2 (2020): 12–17.

Official Website of Hohai University. https://hhu.edu.cn/.

Official Website of Shaanxi Jinghui Canal Irrigation Center. http://www.sxjhj.cn.

Official Website of the Chinese Academy of Engineering. http://www.cae.cn/cae/html/main/index.html.

Official Website of the Chinese Academy of Sciences. http://casad.cas.cn/.

Official Website of Wushan County People's Government Official Website. http://cqws.gov.cn/.

Pan, Jing. *Hohai University*. Nanjing: Hohai University Press, 2015.

Popular Science China. "Qian Ning: Returning Home after Study to Regulate Rivers with Sediments of His Motherland." Accessed on April 18th, 2021. https://tech.gmw.cn/scientist/201512/06/content_17958533.htm.

Qian, Weichang, and Zhou Ganzhi. *An Overview of the Academic Achievements of Eminent Chinese Scientists in the 20th Century · Civil, Hydraulic and Construction Engineering Volume: Volume II*. Beijing: Science Press, 2015.

Ren, Leyun. "Looking into the Sky of Science, Fame and Profit Are as Light as Dust: Remembering Wang Wenshao, an Academician of Chinese Academy of Sciences from China Institute of Water Resources and Hydropower Research." *China Water Resources News*, May 28th, 2010, 7.

Shi, Tingxiu. "Zhang Weixuan: A Deep Love for the Earth." Accessed on April 18th, 2021. https://news.whu.edu.cn/info/1005/24806.htm.

Tan, Guangming. "The University Professor in My Eyes: Commemorating the 100th Anniversary of Professor Zhang Ruijin's Birth." Accessed on April 8th, 2021. http://alumni.whu.edu.cn/info/1041/12721.htm.

Tang, Ting. "Chen Houqun: A Life of Chasing Dreams and Writing Articles on the Dam." *Science and Technology Daily*, January 13th, 2021, 1.

Tang Yaoyuan. "Aspire to Solve River Sedimentation: Professor Xie Jianheng, an Academician of the Chinese Academy of Engineering and Doctoral Supervisor of Wuhan University of Water Resources and Electric Power." *Policy*, no. 3 (1998): 46–47.

The Editorial Board. *Essays and Articles of Mr. Zuo Dongqi*. Nanjing: Hohai University Press, 2019.

The Editorial Board. *Supplement to the River Regulation Work of Zhang Hanying*. Zhengzhou: Yellow River Water Conservancy Press, 2012.

Tian, Lingyan. "Grasp the Major Frontier Topics and Conduct In-depth and Down-to-earth: Interview with Han Qiwei, Academician of Chinese Academy of Engineering." *Chinese Water Conservancy*, no. 21 (2008): 21–22, 11.

Tian, Lingyan and Yang Hua. "Dedicated Research and Persistent Exploration for Furthering the continuous progress in Hydraulic Technology: Interview with Chen Zuyu, Academician of Chinese Academy of Sciences." *China Water Conservancy*, no. 21 (2008): 25–26.

Tian, Lingyan and Yang Hua. "Scientific Researchers Should Prioritize the Urgent Needs of the Country: Interview with Chen Zhikai, Academician of the Chinese Academy of Engineering." *Chinese Water Conservancy*, no. 21 (2008): 19–20.

Tianjin Science Association. "Crossing the Blue Hills Adds Nothing to One's Years: Cao Chusheng, the Famous Water Conservancy Expert." *Science Association Forum*, no. 4 (2001): 12–13.

Wang, Guanglun. *Love for the Mountains and Rivers: A Biography of Zhang Guangdou*. Beijing: China Science and Technology Press, 2014.

Wang, Jianzhu. "Qian Zhengying: Passion for Water Conservancy." Accessed on April 18th, 2021. http://www.cae. cn/cae/html/main/col36/201405/09/20140509163216322423641.html.

Wang, Xue. "Zhang Weizhen: A Major Figure in Percolation Theory at Home and Abroad." *China Science News,* August 1st, 2016: 8.

Wu, Lin and Du Jia. "Lin Gao, the Ninety-year-old Academician: 'Aim for Higher Peaks.'" *Guangming Daily*, November 18th, 2019: 1.

Xu, Deping. "Crossing the Rivers Adds Nothing to One's Years: Interview with Liang Yingchen, an Expert in Waterway and Port Engineering and Academician of the Chinese Academy of Engineering." *Chinese Scientific Awards*, no. 2 (2006): 36–40.

Yan, Li. "Love Sows in Three Gorges: Remembering Liu Guangrun, Academician of Chinese Academy of Engineering." *Policy*, no. 3 (2002): 56–57.

Youheng. "Dedication of Youth and Wisdom to Three Gorges: Remembering Professor Liu Guangrun, Academician of Chinese Academy of Engineering." *Science Enlightenment*, no. 3 (2000): 4–5.

Zeng, Hongjun and Zhang Jin. "The Decision of 'Chaoran': The Former Chief Engineer of China Three Gorges Corporation, Academician Zhang Chaoran." *Contemporary Power Culture*, no. 3 (2015): 38–41.

Zhang, Duo. "'My Youth Is Inseparable from My Motherland, the Youth Story of Wang Sijing, an Academician of the Chinese Academy of Engineering." Accessed on April 20th, 2021. https://baijiahao.baidu.com/s?id=1599538606844107686&wfr=spider&for=pc.

Zhang, Guanyun. "Passion for the Landscape, Devotion to the Oasis: Lei Zhidong, Academician of Chinese Academy of Engineering and Professor of Tsinghua University." *Science and Technology and Industrialization of Chinese Universities*, no. 5 (2008): 45–47

Zhang, Lixian. "Interpreting Gezhouba." Accessed on April 20th, 2021.

https://you.ctrip.com/travels/yichang313/3014148.html.

Zhang, Zhifeng. "Wu Tongju, the Expert in Water Conservancy." *Jiangsu Local Chronicles*, no. 3 (2010): 49–51.

Zheng, Dajun. *The Stars Shine Brightly*. Nanjing: Hohai University Press, 2002.

Zhao, Jiwei, et al. *From Red Soil to Loess: A Biography of Zhu Xianmo*. Beijing: China Science and Technology Press, 2013.

Zhao, Ying. "Academician Lingao: My heart Is with the Dam." Accessed on April 20th, 2021. https://news.sciencenet. cn/htmlnews/2008/11/212807.html? id=212807.

Zhou, Junliang. *Autobiography of Zhou Junliang*. Beijing: Science Press, 2018.